The Purposes of Adult Education

A Short Introduction

The Purposes of Adult Education

A Short Introduction

SECOND EDITION

Bruce Spencer
Athabasca University

TEP

THOMPSON EDUCATIONAL PUBLISHING, INC.
Toronto

Information on how to obtain copies of this book may be obtained from:

Website:	http://www.thompsonbooks.com
E-mail:	publisher@thompsonbooks.com
Telephone:	(416) 766–2763
Fax:	(416) 766–0398

Library and Archives Canada Cataloguing in Publication

Spencer, Bruce /The purposes of adult education : a short introduction / Bruce Spencer. — 2nd ed.

Includes bibliographical references and index.
ISBN-13: 978-1-55077-161-9
ISBN-10: 1-55077-161-2

1. Adult education—Textbooks. 2. Adult education—Canada—Textbooks. I. Title.

LC5215.S63 200   374   C2006-902136-8

Cover design: Margaret Anderson and Tibor Choleva.

Every reasonable effort has been made to acquire permission for copyrighted materials used in this book and to acknowledge such permissions accurately. Any errors or omissions called to the publisher's attention will be corrected in future printings. We acknowledge the support of the Government of Canada through the Book Publishing Industry Development Program for our publishing activities.

Printed in Canada. 1 2 3 4 5   09 08 07 06

Table of Contents

Overview

Welcome to *The Purposes of Adult Education*. The primary aim of this book is to introduce you to the foundations and purposes of adult education. The book provides you with an overview of adult education theory and practice. It explores education for adults, economy, transformation, diversity, and the twenty-first century.

Chapter 1 introduces and reviews education for adults. It summarizes different explanations of the purposes of adult education. It critically reflects on:

- "andragogy" as a description of adult education,
- the foundations of adult education, and
- adult education as a field of practice and as a movement.

Chapter 1 also considers to what extent the study of adult education is centred on "practical knowledge" or on a study of foundational disciplines such as philosophy and history. Having considered the diverse meanings and purposes of adult education, it discusses historical examples of Canadian adult education practice and debates how they should be interpreted.

Next the book examines two distinct areas of adult education purpose: education for economy (Chapter 2) and education for transformation (Chapter 3). Education for economy reviews human capital theory, worker education and training, and new human resource management including workplace learning. It also includes a description of a model of worker-ownership—the Mondragon co-operatives. This serves as a prelude to a debate between "worker co-operation or worker co-operatives" as an objective of adult learning.

Chapter 3 switches attention to the arguments for perspective transformation, Critical Theory, and education for social change. It briefly discusses the work of Jack Mezirow, Jürgen Habermas, Paulo Freire, Myles Horton and examples of British and Canadian community education. It concludes with a review of the claims of old and new social movements as learning sites and debates which of these should be considered as agents of social change.

This is followed by an introduction to the diverse field of adult education (Chapter 4). It recognizes that diverse audiences require diverse purposes and considers what this means for women in adult education. Labour education is chosen as an example for closer scrutiny. It is used to debate whether or not all adult education has to be formal vocational training/education or if it can serve diverse and even opposite purposes.

The book concludes with a brief review of adult education in the twenty-first century (Chapter 5). It considers the economic and technological drive to concentrate educational development on computer-mediated communications offered by distance education. The chapter reviews the experience of distance education as a vehicle for adult education and debates the efficacy of distance education as social adult education. This chapter also serves as a review of the purposes of adult education.

The book is focused on Canadian and North American adult education but also considers global perspectives and experience. It aims to relate your knowledge and experience to the knowledge base of Canadian adult education. The commentary becomes less directional as you progress through the guide. You are encouraged to initiate your own reading on the issues discussed and select topics that interest you for further reading and research.

While the book can be read as a stand-alone text, it is not intended as a comprehensive examination of all adult education. It will provide you with a basis for study of other texts in adult education and related fields. In particular it is designed to accompany *Contexts of Adult Education: Canadian Perspectives* (Fenwick et al., 2006) and *The Foundations of Adult Education in Canada*, Second Edition (Selman et al., 1998).

This book will help you to:

- develop a critical understanding of the foundations of adult education;
- understand some of the major purposes of adult education;
- relate some of the theories of adult education to practice;
- discuss the impact of social, economic and political change on adult education; and
- link discourse on adult education to developments in computer-mediated communication and distance education.

Acknowledgments

This brief book has grown out of my recent teaching about the foundations of adult education to students at the University of Alberta and to distance education on-line students at Athabasca University. It draws on my 30 years of experience as an adult educator in Britain and Canada working in further education (community colleges), the Workers' Educational Association, university adult and continuing education, and university distance education. The examples used in the text inevitably reflect my interest in workers' education.

The structure for this book took shape after discussions with Jennifer Kelly and Derek Briton, both education graduate students at the University of Alberta at the time, and in response to the practical demands of planning a course which would frame adult education in a meaningful way for students who may have some experience in the field but are new to its study. This underlines Freire's argument that in the "dialogical" method of adult education, students are teachers of the teacher at the same time as the teacher is a student of the students.

The purpose was to avoid a simple descriptive overview—with an emphasis on the technical professional focus favoured by many introductory courses and texts—and to present a discussion that previews and analyzes adult education, setting the exploration of adult education within a discourse as to its different purposes and underlying rationale. This rationale has been described in many different ways, but its essence is perhaps best captured by Eduard Lindeman's insistence that above all "adult education is social"—social in its purpose and not just in its process, supportive of social movements and participatory democracy, and it is an education for life, not just for a living. Adult education, it is argued, is forged in practice and in intelligent enquiry.

I am also in debt to Keith Thompson, whose experience of publishing in the field of adult education persuaded me to see the book's structure as sufficiently novel to be worthy of wider distribution and as complementary to his other publications.

1
Education for Adults

A basic tenet of adult education is that since adult students come to the "classroom" with considerable life experience, adult education should build upon that experience. A problem facing a textual discussion about adult education, which wishes to use adult education techniques, is how to replicate an adult education class on paper. How can a text be experiential and encourage interaction between student and student, and between student experience and text?

If you are reading this text as part of a course on adult education, it will be possible to share experiences with fellow students, discuss questions and develop common answers to issues raised. In other circumstances, you may wish to discuss some questions with friends, colleagues or family. Either way, you are asked to see this text as an opportunity to study, discuss and argue. You are encouraged to share the reading experience with others. This book is an invitation to test your own experience and knowledge against the experience and knowledge of others.

What Is the Purpose of Adult Education?

This first chapter focuses on the question, "What is the purpose of adult education?" In doing so, it considers the foundations of adult education, andragogy and the field of adult education. It also looks at the range of provision of adult education/learning by examining the terms, formal, non-formal, and informal education. A review of philosophies of adult education and a debate on how to interpret historical examples of Canadian adult education complete this first chapter.

Selman et al., in *The Foundation of Adult Education*, Second Edition, list four functions for adult education as seen from the individual's viewpoint:

- vocational,
- social,
- recreational, and
- self-developmental (see pp. 29–30 of their text).

They discuss a number of other formulations of the purposes of adult education and then give two listings from other authors (see pp. 31–32). The first is from Jarvis (1985) and is representative of the social view of the aims of adult education. The aims are

- to maintain the social system and reproduce existing social relations;
- to transmit knowledge and reproduce culture;

- for individual advancement and selection;
- to provide for leisure-time pursuit and institutional expansion; and
- to further development and liberation.

Obviously you would have to go back to the original source to see exactly what Jarvis means by these categories, but as you re-read them you may wonder how distinct one is from another. For example, the first two would essentially seem to be saying the same thing—one purpose of adult education is "reproduction" (of culture and society).

The second list comes from Darkenwald and Merriam (1982); Selman et al. comment that this list combines both the personal and social functions of adult education:

- cultivation of the intellect;
- individual self-actualization;
- personal and social improvement;
- social transformation; and
- organizational effectiveness.

We will examine this list again in the philosophy section of this introductory chapter, but there is one issue we should contemplate at this juncture. To the extent that it is true that these American authors (Darkenwald and Merriam) are more concerned with the personal, even when discussing the social, than is Jarvis (who is from Britain), this may itself reflect cultural norms. American society places more emphasis on individualism than does British society—where social forces are more readily acknowledged as powerful. Canadian society is sometimes described as "communitarian" (emphasizing community rather than social class). Therefore, when we read a text, we also have to read a context.

Selman and his coauthors go on to explain another way of grouping the different types of adult education provision at the end of their book (pp. 410ff.): "As we look to the future, it is possible to discern several main clusters or groupings of adult education services." The three groups they identify are

- academic, credential and vocational;
- personal interest and development; and
- social action and social change.

This way of grouping of the different types of adult education is particularly useful because it links this discussion of the aims and purposes with our later discussion of state support of adult education. They argue that government funding is concentrated on the first category and that, while publicly funded agencies may be involved on a cost-recovery basis in the second, they have withdrawn from the third.

Other writers describe the purposes of education as being:

- for reproduction (of the culture, society);
- for economy (to prepare people for work); and
- for transformation/social action (to help bring about societal change).

The first purpose might be concerned with citizenship and order and maintaining culture; the second with investing in human capital, training and human resource development; and the third may focus on both individual transformation and social change.

There are obviously a number of overlaps in these various categories and other writers have expressed the distinctions differently. For example:

- reproduction could be labelled "conservative" (including education for economy, as above);
- the concern with personal improvement and knowledge might be labelled "liberal;" and
- education for social change is often referred to as "radical/ transformational."

It could be argued that, in terms of outcomes, both conservative and liberal education are accommodative/adaptive (they have the essential purpose of adapting and accommodating citizens to the status quo), and therefore education (including adult education) could be depicted as either accommodative/adaptive or transformational.

What Are the Foundations of Adult Education?

At this stage, you do not need a definitive answer to this question. You should, however, have some understanding of the aims and purposes of education, and in particular adult education. To some extent, the answer to this kind of question is found in the practice of adult education. In fact, the theory of adult education—or the foundation of adult education—is grounded in practice. When Lindeman was writing about adult education in the 1920s, 30s and 40s, he was basing his understandings on his practice. The same can be argued for the 1919 Report (Adult Education Committee of the Ministry of Reconstruction 1918–19, UK) which began with a discussion of "The History of Adult Education since 1800," and for many of the more recent seminal works in adult education including those of Freire (1970) and Knowles (1973). This is also clear in some of the contributions to *Contexts of Adult Education: Canadian Perspectives* (Fenwick et al., 2006).

Another approach to understanding the foundations of adult education is to examine all the foundation disciplines such as history, sociology, philosophy and psychology to shed light on the aims and purposes of adult education.

Yet another approach is to consider adult education as essentially located within the broader study of education and, as a social activity, social science. Viewed in this way, we might be less concerned with the particular discipline root and more focused on adult education's place in an understanding of the general field of education and social science, including social theory.

These viewpoints do not have to be regarded as mutually exclusive. It is possible, for example, to consider that essentially adult education is rooted in practice and ask philosophical questions as to its purpose and methods. It is also possible to give specific emphasis to particular subject areas—history and sociology/social theory are obvious examples—to underscore an understanding of the essential foundations of adult education.

Also note that adult education, as a social activity, takes place within specific social, political and economic relations, and links with community development questions, both domestically and internationally.

Andragogy

Malcolm Knowles, in his earlier writing, states that the practice of "the science and art of helping adults learn," what he terms "andragogy," is significantly different from traditional school-based instruction, or pedagogy (Knowles, 1973). Knowles sees adults as:

- more self-directed, rather than relying on others for direction; and

- mature and, therefore, experienced, with the experience providing a rich resource for learning.

He also contends that:

- adults' readiness to learn is linked to what they need to know;

- adult orientation to learning is problem centred rather than subject centred; and

- adult motivation to learn is internal (Knowles, 1984).

For Knowles these five features distinguish adult education from the education of children—andragogy from pedagogy. See the table on the next page for a summary of these differences.

Knowles was not the first to use the term andragogy as a description of adult education, nor was he the first to identify these and other distinctions between adult and child education/learning. Knowles was, however, responsible for arguing that adult education should be regarded as andragogy and, as such, clearly distinguished from child education, or pedagogy. He continues to be the most often-cited adult educator in North America; his individualistic and psychological arguments have found a resonance with practising adult educators. This may be testimony to the fact that he has been prepared to adapt his basic arguments in the face of

A COMPARISON OF ASSUMPTIONS AND DESIGNS OF PEDAGOGY AND ANDRAGOGY

	Pedagogy	Andragogy
Assumptions		
Self-concept	Dependency	Increasing self-directedness
Experience	Of little worth	Learners are a rich source for learning
Readiness	Biological development, social pressure	Developmental tasks of social roles
Time perspective	Postponed application	Immediacy of application
Orientation to learning	Subject-oriented	Problem-centred
Design Element		
Climate	Authority-oriented Formal Competitive	Mutuality Respectful Collaborative Informal
Planning	By teacher	Mechanism for mutual planning
Diagnosis of need	By teacher	Mutual self-diagnosis
Formulation of objectives	By teacher	Mutual negotiation
Design	Logic of the subject matter Content units	Sequenced in terms of readiness Problem units
Activities	Transmittal techniques	Experiential techniques (inquiry)
Evaluation	By teacher	Mutual re-diagnosis of needs Mutual measurement of program

Source: From Knowles, M. (1984). *The Adult Learner: A Neglected Species* (3rd Ed.), Houston: Gulf, p. 116.

criticism. For example, he moved away from the idea that andragogy and pedagogy were polar opposites, and he has not made too grandiose a claim for his argument as an all-embracing theory of adult education. The acceptance of his ideas may also reflect the desire in the United States, at the time, for a theory to underscore the growing practice of adult education/training, a theory which most practitioners could subscribe to and use. It would also distinguish teachers of adults from teachers of children.

The question remains, however, as to whether adult education should be considered "andragogy," and whether or not this is a useful contribution to understanding adult education. In Europe, where the term andragogy is widely used, andragogy is considered a part of pedagogy, the part which deals with adults. Another way of looking at it is to see to what extent the practice of adult education has grown out of our understanding of pedagogy. In Britain, for example, the Plowden Report, *Children and their Primary Schools*, 1967 (reporting on elementary schooling), was central in bringing forward a "child-centred" pedagogy which advocated problem-centred learning strategies with pupil choice, discovery project work and other techniques which Knowles subsequently labelled "andragogical" (there is no evidence that Knowles was aware of the Plowden committee's work). This work in schools influenced British adult education practice, specifically the classroom methods used for teaching adults from the mid-1970s on.

In the United States, too, a number of school teachers contacted Knowles to tell him they had been using progressive educational methods for some time, but, although he acknowledged this in his later writing, he still referred to those teachers as using "andragogical methods" (Knowles in Athabasca University, 1988). Knowles does, however, make it clear that he now sees that pedagogy and andragogy "are not two opposed models or assumptions, but rather parallel" (Athabasca University, 1988, p. 3).

Many adult education scholars would argue that Knowles's definition of adult education as andragogy justifies an individualistic and psychological approach to adult education based exclusively on an analysis of the characteristics of the learner. This approach misses entirely the arguments of others, such as Lindeman, one of Knowles's own mentors, that "true adult education is social," and that "there is adult education and there is education for adults" and they should not be conflated (Lindeman, 1947, p. 55). According to this view, Knowles's approach is focused on individual adult learning and, though apparently radical, it can be seen as innately conservative justifying all adult training and adult learning that uses the features he identified as "andragogy." Andragogy applies regardless of the purpose or outcome of the education provision for adults. According to these critics, andragogy is essentially "education for adults," not "adult education;" it is stripped of social purpose.

Therefore, while Knowles has helped distinguish the education of adults from that of children (keep in mind that the teaching techniques used in both school and adult classes are parallel and overlap), his focus on andragogy (on adults and adult learning) misses out on an understanding of adult education as a distinctive social activity. This social activity may be considered as outside of mainstream post-secondary provision of further and higher education for adults. Knowles can also be held to downplay the radical context of progressive adult education—for example, the emphasis on co-operative rather than competitive learning and on knowledge as a product of social discourse and activity as much as it is of text.

However, in this book, we will be considering the whole range of what is popularly understood as adult education or adult learning. This ranges from vocational training to social purpose education, from provision in post-secondary institutions to education within social movements.

The Field of Adult Education

Our consideration of andragogy—of adult education and learning—does raise a number of other questions that help us explore the field of adult education. The focus on adult experience, on the recognition of the value of experiential learning, and on the purposes and forms of adult education leads to questions such as:

- Is all learning "good"?
- Is all experience unproblematic?
- What kind of adult education should be promoted in a liberal democracy?
- What distinctions can be drawn between formal, non-formal and informal adult education, and do these help us identify what adult education is?
- Can adult education be seen as a "movement"?

The answers to these questions are explored in the following discussion.

Experiential Learning

Alan Thomas commented that "education floats on a sea of learning." He points out that learning is going on all the time and that structured education is but a small part of it (Thomas, 1991). However, while we should acknowledge that this learning exists, would we want to argue that all learning is "good" or that the purposes to which learning is put are socially beneficial? For example, is it good that people learn how to use cocaine or how to con pensioners out of their savings? Lists of good and bad learning might differ, but only a purist would argue that all learning is inherently "good" or, more specifically, that learning should be seen as a value-free activity.

Experience can be very problematic. People may have to "unlearn" racism or abusive behaviour—for example, some males have to "unlearn" their violent behaviour towards women, or people may have to overcome their particular experiences before they can learn tolerance or co-operative behaviour. Experience is also constantly being interpreted, by individuals and by others. The same experience can lead to radically different conclusions. Although experience is a starting point for adult education, and experiential learning is seen by some as the essence of adult education, experience still remains problematic. The challenge for adult educators is to draw from and connect to student experience in ways that allow for development and growth both individually and socially (aiding the principles of democracy and civil society). Students have to use socially learned knowledge, but at the same time, not be limited by their experiences.

State Support

If education in general reflects society, then so, too, does adult education. All education will reflect the current norms and values of political economy. For example, there is the current emphasis on training and retraining, reflecting the demand that adult education must meet the needs of the economy. This mirrors the concerns of neo-conservative governments for a more skilled workforce that is equipped to compete with others in the global marketplace. The argument that governments have to cut public spending and concentrate resources on core activity also fits neatly with this philosophy. There are no resources, the argument goes, to subsidize liberal adult education; it can only be undertaken on a cost-recovery basis. In short, in this analysis, adult education equals job training.

This narrow interpretation of the state support that can be expected does not apply universally. It can be argued that a liberal, democratic state should fund diverse educational activity reflecting the pluralist nature of liberal democracy. An example of this argument can be found in the 1919 Report:

> It is said that the educational work of sectarian bodies ought not to be subsidised out of public funds. We do not agree; in our judgment whether the State ought to help such education depends upon the quality of the work and not upon the institution which conducts it. Any other standard puts the State in a position of censorship which it ought not to be expected to take. It would inevitably give rise to a differentiation between the knowledge which in the opinion of the State is desirable to disseminate and the diffusion of which should not be encouraged.
>
> The State could, indeed, hardly avoid the charge of "manufacturing public opinion." In our view the only sound principle is that the State should be willing to help all serious educational work, including the educational work of institutions and organizations which are recruited predominantly from students with, say, a particular religious or political philosophy (Wiltshire, 1980, p. 20).

This approach has generally guided the funding of adult education in the Scandinavian countries, and to a lesser extent historically in Canada, with differing religious and social groupings receiving state support. But we should recognize the importance of this statement and acknowledge that today adult education is not being broadly supported. Consequently, governments could be accused of "manufacturing public opinion" rather than supporting a plurality of opinion.

It can be argued that the 1919 Report was a product of its time. It reflected

- some recognition for the contribution of working people to winning the war;
- the strength of radical ideas and events;
- a desire to incorporate radicalism within the mainstream of political life; and
- the balance of class forces which favoured concessions to labour.

On the other hand, it could be argued that the report expressed a genuine "liberalism," a model of state behaviour which should guide liberal democracy.

One interpretation of Scandinavian support for this perspective could emphasize the extent of the power of organized labour and social democracy within those countries—the balance of class forces favours state support— while another might emphasize the entrenched commitment to liberal democracy and a welfare state sustained over a long period of time. Both arguments point in the same direction: Only where there is a commitment (either genuine or forced) to the principles of liberal democracy can we expect the state to support diverse adult education provisions. In other cases, the state support will generally (though perhaps not exclusively) reflect entrenched economic interests. We should, therefore, not be so surprised to find a shift to economic liberalism (neo-conservative, global market economics), resulting in a narrowing of adult education provision to serve economic goals. The modern state's support for "lifelong learning" does not reflect the 1919 Report's or Lindeman's perspective of "education for life, not for living." Rather, it reflects the reverse—a continual emphasis on training and retraining and a neglect of the "lifeworld" (see Welton, 1995).

"Sites" of Learning: Formal, Non-formal and Informal Education

Many authorities currently define all post-secondary education as adult education, or as an "adult learning system" (Alberta Advanced Education and Career Development, 1994). With this definition, adult education loses its distinctiveness. One way of making some distinction within the field is to identify the various "sites" where learning takes place.

- **Formal education** carries credentials, has a set curriculum, and is usually provided by an educational institution. In many cases formal education is more accurately described as further or higher education (or generally "post-secondary") and is linked to achieving vocational or academic credentials.

- **Non-formal education** is organized by educational or other institutions or groups. It is usually non-credential (essentially non-credit), part-time, delivered via linked weekends, day or week-long schools, and targeted to satisfy individual, recreational, organizational or social objectives. It is what we have always understood adult education to be.

- **Informal education** is more often described as informal learning. It is the learning that goes on all the time, individually and in groups. For example, a local environmental action group (or individuals in the group) might learn how to organize meetings, prepare submissions or write newsletters as an integral part of their group activities. All of these are examples of informal learning.

If the group puts on a day-school for themselves or the public, they are then structuring an educational event—an example of non-formal education. If a member signs up for a course on "toxic waste disposal" offered by the local college, perhaps as part of a waste management program, the member may be considered as entering formal education.

While the non-formal educational provision for adults might be considered "adult education" in the traditional sense, the above example illustrates how different kinds of adult learning can be connected. In this book we will continue to consider the range of formal, non-formal and informal adult education and learning as "adult education." While recognizing the strength of the argument that true "adult education is social," that is, it has a social purpose, and that we should distinguish between "education for adults and adult education," the term adult education will be used to cover all education for adults. (See Selman et al., pp. 25–26 for further discussion of formal, non-formal and informal education.)

Adult Education as a Movement

There is one last introductory question to address. To what extent can we refer to adult education as a movement?

Selman et al. (see p. 15) refer to adult education as a movement. This same theme is scattered throughout the adult education literature. When the 1919 Report reviewed the practice of adult education at the time and looked at the social and religious groups promoting adult education, it reported on adult education as "a field of practice" and as "a movement."

It argued that the thrust of the adult education provision was emancipatory, an "education for life" not just "for livelihood." It also argued that there were common goals of enlightenment and participatory citizenship. Others, such as Lindeman, writing in the interwar period, also emphasized adult education's goal as one of promoting democracy. Thus, adult education, although diverse and in some cases involving competing groups, could be depicted as a movement, that is, enjoying a commonality of purpose and a direction.

How does this description fit today? If the field of adult education refers to all adult education and training, including vocational and workplace learning, post-secondary provision, credentialized and non-credentialized, it is difficult to view adult education as a movement. Today's diverse goals reflect some fundamentally opposed philosophies and values (we can see these in our discussion below of workplace learning and new human-resource-management practices); it is not at all clear that most adult education today is geared towards emancipation and democracy. We should not abandon the idea that adult education can provide critical reflection and empowerment. However, another way of looking at this issue is to consider that adult education today is best understood as a process which can aid other social movements.

Philosophies of Adult Education

Earlier, we argued that the purposes of adult education can be discovered through an examination of practice. While this might be the preferred route, it is also possible to approach the question from a "foundational discipline" perspective.

Elias and Merriam (1980) identified six philosophies of adult education:

- **Liberal**. This philosophy emphasizes a concern with the liberal arts, a love of learning, and developing intellectual powers.
- **Progressive**. Following Dewey, this philosophy encompasses reason, experience and feeling. Education is a social activity and has a purpose. The majority of North American adult educators subscribe to a progressive view.
- **Behaviourist**. Education is seen as having definite behavioural objectives, being linked to skill training, planning and evaluation. It is competency-based.
- **Humanistic**. This approach emphasizes the autonomy of the individual, the present, freedom and dignity. It has been associated with self-directed learning and human-resource development.

- **Radical**. This sees education as a means for consciousness-raising and for social change.
- **Analytical**. Following Paterson and Lawson, this philosophy argues for seeing the aims of education more in terms of its effect on the individual and its utility to the individual and less in terms of its social implications.

Elias and Merriam revised their list in 1984—"analytical" was subsumed into "liberal"—reducing their original list of six to five.

These six philosophies of adult education have been widely used and refined by others. Darkenwald and Merriam (1982), in a reading referred to above, switched to conclude with five emphases drawn from a consideration of the differing aims of adult education—cultivation of the intellect, personal development, progressiveness, radicalness, and organizational effectiveness. It is worth quoting their conclusion at length:

> This chapter has attempted to present an overview of the philosophies of adult education. The differing aims of adult education provide a focus for organizing the diverse philosophical writings. Five emphases were discussed, with their respective views on content, the role of the teacher and learner, and the nature of the instructional process.
>
> The cultivation of the intellect is one objective of adult education. Proponents of this view conceive of adult education as a neutral activity divorced from social action. A curriculum emphasizing liberal studies and a traditional view of the teacher-student interaction characterizes this approach.
>
> Personal development constitutes a second emphasis in adult education. Drawing from humanistic and existential orientations, educators with this bias see adult education as concerned primarily with promoting individual growth and development. A by-product of this emphasis will be benefits to society. Content thus becomes whatever promotes individual growth, the student is the focus of the process, and group interaction is the favoured instructional mode.
>
> Perhaps the major proportion of American educational philosophers reflect the progressive view of adult education. Here the aim of adult education is both personal development and social progress. Content is drawn from life situations, the preferred method is problem solving, and teachers and learners are partners in the task of learning.
>
> In direct opposition to the proponents of "neutral knowledge" are those who advocate radical social change through adult education. Here education is viewed as value-laden and never neutral. Content comes from the consciousness of the oppressed and the disadvantaged, the teacher is also a learner, and the methodology is a dialogical encounter that leads to praxis—that is, reflective thought and action.
>
> Finally, organizational effectiveness is the aim of a large segment of American adult education. Public and private sector organizations strive to become more efficient deliverers of goods or services. To this end, they may engage their employees in training, education, or development activities characterized by a variety of purposes and instructional methodologies (Darkenwald and Merriam, 1982, p. 69).

It might help you to conceptualize the philosophical approaches if you try to put the different adult educators that you have read about under different headings. For example:

- **Progressive**. The progressive school has the most disciples in North America—Eduard Lindeman, Adelaide Hoodless, Malcolm Knowles, Edward Corbett, Moses Coady, Roby Kidd and Alan Thomas may all be listed here.

- **Humanistic**. Knowles could also be included in the humanistic philosophy along with Abraham Maslow, Allen Tough and Carl Rogers.

- **Radical**. The radical grouping could encompass Paulo Freire, Antonio Gramsci, Watson Thomson and Violet McNaughton. But should it also include Coady and Lindeman?

At this point, it might be enlightening to reflect on Anatole France's quote with which Lindeman begins his Foreword to *The Meaning of Adult Education* (1926): "Each of us must even be allowed to possess two or three philosophies at the same time." Lindeman interprets this for the purpose "of saving our thought from the deadly formality of consistency."

An alternative view of the categorizing of the purpose of adult education can be found in the way the term "liberal adult education" is used in Britain. In the "great tradition" of pre-1945 adult education (particularly, in the Workers' Educational Association and university extra-mural work), liberal adult education came to mean: "liberal humane studies, particularly social studies, non-vocational courses, education for reflective citizenship and a special focus on serving the working class" (Spencer and McIlroy, 1991).

In recent times, "liberal adult education" has continued to be defined as inclusive of both traditional liberal education and radical perspectives. It encompasses "social action," "community education" and "social purpose" education (Taylor, Rockhill and Fieldhouse, 1985). Its broad usage has been contested by North American scholars (e.g. Brookfield, 1986) who generally have a more restricted view of "liberal" adult education (essentially interpreted as liberal studies or liberal arts), but it remains viable in Britain.

As a student of adult education, this later discussion may confuse you as to the distinctiveness of different philosophies of adult education and how to distinguish between different types of provision. However, this discussion illustrates that the purposes of adult education should be viewed within a social and historical context. Other examples could be provided from other countries. For example, in Nepal, the term non-formal education is used widely to describe all non-school education. The main thrust of this work is literacy training, and participants include adults and young persons, many of whom have experienced little formal schooling and accept adult responsibilities at an early age. For example, a 14-year-old would not be exceptional in a Nepalese adult education class, but would be considered out of place in a Canadian adult class.

The purpose of this foray into philosophies is to provide you with alternative ways of looking at adult education. You can then begin to make your own categories and explain your own approaches to the practice of adult education.

Historical Examples of Canadian Adult Education

As argued earlier, another approach to discovering the aims and purposes of adult education is to look at actual practice. We can do this by examining historical examples of Canadian adult education.

We are going to explore these historical examples by reviewing the arguments that historians have offered to interpret these events. In particular, we will debate the issues raised by the contributors to *Knowledge for the People*, edited by Welton (1987). This collection of essays stimulated a renewed interest in adult education history and excited the imagination of many students of adult education. We will debate how to interpret four historical examples of adult education: Mechanics' Institutes, Women's Institutes, Frontier College and the Antigonish Movement.

Welton's introduction to *Knowledge for the People* raises a number of issues about the nature of history. One point he misses, however, is that the movement towards a new history, a social history rooted in ordinary people's experience, essentially grew out of adult education classes as did the broader cultural studies (McIlroy and Westwood, 1993). The first generally acknowledged new history text was that of E.P. Thompson, *The Making of the English Working Class*, published in 1963, which was written when Thompson was teaching adult students in liberal adult education classes while in the Extra-Mural Department of the University of Leeds in the 1950s and 60s (Goodway, 1996).

For the moment, we will concentrate on two questions raised in Welton's discussion:

- What was the purpose of education—was it social change or accommodation?
- How much control did the learners ("the people") have over the provision/institutions?

As Selman et al. point out in Chapters 2 and 3 of *The Foundations of Adult Education in Canada*, there were a number of external influences on Canadian (including Quebec) adult education and there were specific Canadian responses to Canadian conditions. We will start by looking at a British import, the Mechanics' Institutes. We will then move on to consider two Canadian responses to the emerging frontier/immigrant/ farming nation—the Women's Institutes and Frontier College. This history section will conclude with Canada's most renowned (perhaps more so outside of Canada than within) adult education initiative, the Antigonish Movement.

Mechanics' Institutes, 1827–1890s

Mechanics' Institutes were created in Britain as a means of providing scientific and technical information for workers, especially skilled workers or "mechanics." As has been argued by Robins in Welton's *Knowledge for the People*, these tradesmen knew how to carry out the procedures of their trades, but frequently had no opportunity to learn the scientific background or the "why" of those procedures. The Institutes started with a mixture of self-help and philanthropic motivation. Mechanics' Institutes were experimented with as early as 1800 in Edinburgh, but the movement did not begin in earnest until the foundation of the London Mechanics' Institution in the 1820s. (Over the years, the Institutes in Britain, like those in Canada, strayed from their original purpose and became general cultural organizations.)

In 1827 an Institute was established in Toronto. The following year, Institutes were started in Halifax and Montreal. Institutes were set up in British Columbia as well but not until the early 1860s. The Institutes were most developed in Ontario—there were 311 of them by 1895. The Department of Education in Ontario even saw the Institutes as the chief agency through which "the upgrading of workers in the technical arts could be achieved" (F. Vernon, 1960, p. 481).

Women's Institutes (WI)

Even in rural areas, women were often divided by politics, religion and language. As argued by Dennison (Welton, 1987), one of the few organizations which admitted all women was the Women's Institute (WI). The WI was initiated in Stoney Creek, Ontario, in 1897, by Adelaide Hoodless, a woman well known in Ontario for her campaign—following the death of her son—for clean milk.

The formation of the British Columbia Women's Institute came as a direct result of the BC Farmers' Institute's efforts to provide speakers on topics of interest to their members' wives. The talks were so popular that the provincial government decided to organize Women's Institutes throughout the province. By the end of 1909, sixteen institutes had been organized. In 1911, the government gave them statutory authority and provided funding.

Each geographical area was suited to different types of agriculture and women were, therefore, divided by geography, type of work, and market practices. In isolated farms and small communities, women welcomed the opportunity to get out and meet other women. Education and community have always been at the heart of WI activity.

The focus of the Institutes was on "homemaking," including household crafts and child-rearing, and topics of local interest, including aspects of farm management. Women also exchanged views about more worldly issues. For example, two legal areas which aroused widespread concern among publicly minded women were guardianship laws and married women's property rights. In western Canada, mothers didn't become legal parents until after the First World War. Before that, a father was empowered to manage his children's property, collect their income and determine their religion and education. The law made it clear that the father was the sole and unchallenged parent. Property rights denied women the right of any return for their work as wives. Unlike the US, Canada did not open home-steads to wives or single women. Only if she was the head of a household could a woman, like any male over age 18, earn title to a quarter section of land by farming it. Activists within the Women's Institutes joined other campaigners to bring about changes in these and other laws.

Women's Institutes spread across Canada and were "exported" to the UK and other (primarily British Empire/Commonwealth) countries. An international organization was established under Canadian leadership in the 1930s.

Frontier College

Cook (Welton, 1987) observes that Canadian society at the turn of the last century was guilty, in the words of Alfred Fitzpatrick, of the "crime of the desertion and demoralization of the frontiersman, the crime not only of robbing him of the right of an education, but the equally damnable crime of licensing men and institutions to degrade him." Alfred Fitzpatrick, a social gospeller, made the above charge as he waged war to secure justice for the camp men. His foundation of the Reading Camp Association in 1901, and its evolution into Frontier College, represented a pragmatic response to the human needs of the frontier and to the failure of government to accept responsibility.

Frontier College created the labourer–teacher, one who lived and worked with the students. As a teaching method, this has gained some acceptance in development programs. In Fitzpatrick's day, the frontier condition was most clearly exemplified by Canada's third great wave of railway building, which saw the country's railway lines increase from 15,000 to 40,000 miles between 1891 and 1921. As a result, thousands of largely unskilled and uneducated labourers worked in virtual isolation and were cut off from even the most rudimentary social and educational services that were beginning to be offered in cities and towns.

Frontier College claimed that, in the more stable lumber camps, 50 percent of the men would attend classes; but on the more volatile railway camps, attendance ranged from 2 to 10 percent. The reading "rooms" were used by 90 percent of the literate men (about 50 percent of the camp). Cook notes the peak of the operations was reached in 1913 when 71 labourer-teachers were placed in camps. By 1919, over 600 instructors, including a small number of women, had served in every province and territory except Prince Edward Island.

Antigonish Movement

This is perhaps the most significant Canadian adult education/community education project. How should it be judged? Is it transformatory? It was seen as an alternative to "socialism" by many sponsors and yet, there certainly were elements of social change. It definitely is an example of adult education as social activity and not just education for adults, to use Lindeman's distinction.

The Antigonish movement was a product of its time and place (not that it could not be replicated in a different form, as indeed it has been in a number of developing countries). Lotz and Welton (Welton, 1987) note that, in the interwar recession years, the Maritimes experienced a long series of depressions and depopulations with no real recovery. As a result, working people were receptive to arguments for alternative ways of creating and organizing work. In the Maritimes, people generally lived in settled communities dependent on farming, fishing and some extraction industry. They accepted the church as playing a key role in their communities. They had also had some experience with co-operative organization where family farms shared the use of equipment, purchase of fertiliser and sale of products.

The leaders of the movement, such as Jimmy Tompkins, had been influenced by Danish folk-schools and believed in a university for the people where knowledge and resources were available to ordinary men and women. His first initiative was to set up "Peoples' Schools," which were traditional liberal adult education classes. The movement leaders also realized the importance of gaining access to local people's savings for reinvestment in their localities. This gave rise to a high priority to founding credit unions.

Perhaps the most significant development which lead to the take-off of the Antigonish Movement was the organization of the fisherman in 1929 by Moses Coady. Tompkins had been influential in establishing a provincial investigation into the semi-feudal economic and social conditions of the industry and, following the commission's report, had pushed for Coady, a Catholic priest, to be given the organizing task. Coady took on the merchants ("fish lords") and cajoled the fishermen into organization, preaching the values of co-operation.

The public meetings and lectures organized by Coady and others at the Extension Department of St Francis Xavier University were followed up with community study clubs/circles that identified community problems and sought solutions in collective actions and co-operative work. In a university publication, "The Antigonish Way," Coady writes:

> The technique was discovered by facing the actual situation and planning a way by which the people of eastern Canada could be mobilized to think, study, and to get enlightenment. We found the discussion circle. This did not involve any teachers. It was in line with our whole co-operative idea. We would make education part of the self-help movement. The people would come together by themselves and discuss problems. The first logical step in this process was for someone to round up the people, so to speak. This involved the mass meeting (1943, p.66, reproduced in Crane, p. 231).

The movement has been described as "education plus organization." It started by identifying and analyzing people's economic problems and then organizing to change those economic conditions.

Conclusion

The history of Canadian adult education illustrates the diversity of educational purpose ranging from education for citizenship and conformity to radical social change, education for accommodation/adaptation and education for transformation. The examples we have looked at are of non-formal and informal education for social and economic purpose; they are essentially examples of education as a social activity with a social purpose—adult education as opposed to just education for adults (with the strongest examples being the Antigonish Movement and the Women's Institutes and the weakest, the Mechanics' Institutes). In terms of educational philosophy, these historical cases can be interpreted as mainly demonstrating elements of progressive, humanist and radical ideas.

Suggested Readings

Parts 1 ("Contexts in Transition") and 2 ("Philosophical and Critical Contexts") in *Contexts of Adult Education: Canadian Perspectives* (Fenwick et al., 2006).

Chapters 1, 2 and 3 of *The Foundations of Adult Education in Canada, Second Edition* (Selman et al., 1998).

Section 1, Part 1 ("Historical and Current Contexts") and Part 2 ("Aims of Adult Education") in *Learning for Life* (Scott et al., 1998).

The Foreword and the first two chapters of Paulo Freire's *Pedagogy of the Oppressed* (1972, re-printed 1990), where he argues for a liberatory adult education. Freire uses these two chapters to frame his argument. Note that Freire does not use the term andragogy; he contrasts traditional pedagogy (what he calls "banking" education) with liberatory education (utilizing problem-posing and dialogical concepts). The Foreword is useful as a summary of some of Freire's key ideas. You may wish to read both the Forward and the two chapters more than once.

Welton, M.R. (Ed.) (1987), *Knowledge for the People*. See the contributions, particularly Welton's Introduction.

Welton, M .R. (2001), *Little Mosie from the Margaree: A Biography of Moses Coady*.

English, Leona (Ed.) (2005), *International Encyclopedia of Adult Education*, provides lots of useful definitions and relevant summaries.

THE MECHANICS' INSTITUTES

Debate: Foster Vernon has argued that "they [Mechanics' Institutes] were essentially a middle class organization run by people with middle class values which they constantly sought to impose on members of the lower class who came to the Institute searching for help with their learning problems" (1960, p. 148). Palmer (1983) suggests that such a generalization distorts as much as it clarifies. He argues that Mechanics' Institutes cannot be divorced from their local context in which the strength of the working class movement would contribute to the vibrancy of the working class presence in these early examples of adult education. We must not, therefore, assume that the control of propertied elements, so common in many institutes, resulted in an acquiescent working class constituency.

Evidence: As has been pointed out, merchants, manufacturers and clerks often controlled local Institutes, while working men used the services and facilities for their own purposes, often expressing distinct dissatisfaction with the policies and practices of the directors. There is also some evidence that meetings took place of the "10 Hours Movement" (a popular radical campaign to restrict the working day to 10 hours) in and around some Institutes, a demand which certainly was opposed by the propertied classes and, therefore, speaks to some independence of some mechanics.

Conclusion: We can conclude, therefore, that the educational activity, the public lectures and the reading rooms were designed to incorporate a segment of the emerging working class into the goals of the new industrial society. While skilled artisans were not in control of their education, they made their own uses of it. They used the resources of the Mechanics' Institutes to support independent actions.

Comment: These early examples of adult education in Canada (starting before the Riel Rebellions and Confederation) spurned other educational initiatives. They were forerunners of university extension lectures and helped establish public libraries.

THE WOMEN'S INSTITUTES

Debate: While the text argues that women took control of their own learning, you should recognize that the BC Women's Institute was sponsored by the BC government to meet some of its objectives. Therefore, an alternative view would be that the WI in BC was not essentially independent, under the control of the learners.

Evidence: The following extract questions WI independence from government:

> In BC Women's Institutes were organized to aid the Government in carrying out its Agricultural policy. The Government policy is defined in the Aims and Objects as contained in the Rules and Regulations, under which all Institutes are organized and no Institute, whether Individual, District or Provincial, can make any change in Rules or Regulations without the consent of the Department" (Country Life in British Columbia, 1925, p. 3).

This article goes on to specify the relevant legislation and to detail the government funding and financial arrangements of the BC Institutes.

Conclusion: The Welton collection suggests that the BC women were engaged in more independent education than the mechanics. This may be a matter of historical interpretation. The above quote illustrates the importance of checking original sources. In this case, it is a question of what weight is given to the formal arrangements of both organizations and to the evidence of independent practice. We have more information about the practices of the BC Institutes than we do about the earlier Mechanics' Institutes. The BC WI was sponsored by government, but it did not prevent some women from using the WI as a base for their campaigns for social change.

Comment: The WI became the largest adult education movement in Canada, but it was not the only one. There were a number of other women's organizations, as Jeff Taylor (1994) has argued: "The independent women's movement that emerged in the last three decades of the nineteenth century in North America created organizational and ideological space for women" (Taylor, 1994 p. 24).

By 1914, a second network of farm women's groups in Alberta and Saskatchewan, with overtly political aims, had been established. The United Farm Women of Alberta (UFWA) and the Women Grain Growers of Saskatchewan (WGGS) were the women's section of the farm protest movement. Though closely associated with the men's farm protest movement, neither the UFWA nor the WGGS thought of themselves as auxiliary; instead they saw themselves as co-combatants in the struggle for economic and social justice. Because of this political stance, the UFWA and the WGGS didn't attract the same breadth of membership as the Women's Institute. The differences in philosophy also had some effect on the activities. The WI women tended towards homemaking and service to their community, whereas the farm movement women delved more overtly into politics and economics province wide. One of the key organizers and educators in Saskatchewan was Violet McNaughton who used a range of educational techniques—from kitchen meetings to journalism and radio.

FRONTIER COLLEGE

Debate: The history of Frontier College is fascinating but ambiguous. The College provided a voice for neglected and exploited campmen, but "justice" was not to be achieved by independent organization (such as trade unions) or by social transformation. The reforms sought were limited in scope and yet were resisted by the state. Therefore, should we consider Frontier College as a site for independent learning?

Evidence: As argued by Cook, most Canadians remained oblivious to the conditions of the camps. As a group, they were largely ignored by the traditional unions, the universities and even the churches. Although Canadian society was churchgoing, it was, in Cook's view, "also a society of unrelieved materialism; Christians with a social conscience were not common." Fitzpatrick felt that the problem was the state's responsibility. He suggested that if the camps were idle intellectually and morally, it would breed social ills and be a menace to the state. By 1910, he warned that "the seeds of revolutionary socialism" were being sown and were "flourishing best in the foreign born seed bed."

It is clear from Cook's account that Fitzpatrick's social purpose was to Canadianize the immigrant campmen by providing education for citizenship. At the same time he believed education should be for all, not for a privileged class alone. Further, the privileged class not only had an obligation to make education available to those less privileged, by offering themselves as teachers, but could learn from them as well.

Conclusion: The education offered was to "incorporate" new immigrants, though the state refused to assist. Frontier College was a voluntary organization but not under the control of the learners. Undoubtedly some workers and labourer–teachers used the opportunity to promote independent learning.

Comment: Today Frontier College focuses on literacy programs in workplaces and prisons (using prisoner teachers) and includes some ESL/FSL courses. It continues to recruit university students for its programs—volunteer literacy tutors—under the banner of the University in Overalls (the title of Fitzpatrick's book, 1920).

THE ANTIGONISH MOVEMENT

Debate: Lotz and Welton make it clear that the Antigonish Movement was moderately successful and could point to a number of concrete achievements. In 1939, there were 19,600 people enrolled in 2,265 study clubs, 342 credit unions and 162 other co-operative ventures in the three Maritime provinces. However, the movement did not achieve Coady's ambition of "transforming society from the margins." It is clear that although there was considerable direction offered by the leaders, the learners had significant control over their learning and social actions—the Antigonish Movement was a social movement, but was it a movement committed to transformation?

Evidence: The answer to this question hinges on your own view as to the possibilities for change within a dominantly capitalist society. This is not just a question of historical interpretation, but also one of socio-political preference. Coady understood that there were powerful vested economic and political interests, which he referred to as "anti social elements," and that the Antigonish Movement, taken to its logical conclusion, would challenge them:

> There is not much hope for the world because the economically and politically powerful people of the Western democracies—and this goes also for religious leaders of all denominations, at least a great percentage of them—will stop short of doing the whole job. Their philosophy is: we will go far enough with reform to ward off the present danger, but we must not allow reform to interfere with the privileged status quo. (Coady, reproduced in Crane p. 237).

Conclusion: Coady's solution was to rely on the people "not being fooled any longer," although it could be argued that his alliances with the state and some capitalists—such as Carnegie—were always going to limit the movement's transformatory potential.

Comment: Although there are significant differences, a number of parallels can be drawn between Freire's methods among the poor of Brazil and those of Coady and his colleagues, specifically in relation to getting people to identify their own problems and building change from the "bottom up" via their own solutions. Both provide good examples of adult education practice, particularly as it is applied to community development, and both are influenced by "Christian socialist" philosophy.

There are also parallels between the attempt to establish co-operatives in the Maritimes and the more integrated co-operatives at Mondragon, northern Spain (which we will examine later). The Antigonish Movement remains an important example of a Canadian adult education response to the desire for a community-controlled, sustainable alternative to corporate globalization, encouraging working people to become, in Coady's words, "masters of their own destiny."

2
Education for Economy

This chapter introduces the arguments and counter-arguments regarding the idea that a principle purpose of adult education is to train and retrain workers and to prepare for work those who are not employed. It first discusses human capital theory as the basis for the current interest in worker training and workplace learning. It then notes the shift of state funding from other forms of adult education to vocational training and the accompanying arguments favouring competency-based training. It examines new human-resource management arguments underpinning workplace learning and contrasts "empowerment" in private and worker-owned enterprise. The model of worker-owned enterprise used in this contrast is that of the Mondragon co-operatives of northern Spain.

This chapter establishes a context against which you can undertake your own reading. It does not provide detailed guidance to all the arguments of "education for economy" or cover all the ground now exposed by the debates on work and education (see Section 2, Part 1, "Education for Economy" of *Learning for Life* in Scott et al., 1998, for more complete coverage). It seeks instead to introduce and set in context a number of topics and to discuss some of the issues, such as the nature of human resource management or co-operative enterprise, which are ignored in much of the literature.

The approach taken in this chapter is in keeping with three adult education objectives, which are

- to open up the text to greater student choice;
- to develop independent learning habits; and
- to allow more space for you to inject your interests and experience into the topic under discussion.

With these objectives in mind, you need to think about the chapters in *Contexts of Adult Education* and other articles or texts that will allow you to follow up the topics that interest you.

Industrial and Post-industrial Societies

As you read about work and learning, you will come across many references suggesting that, compared to a few years ago, we now live in a post-industrial, post-modern or even post-capitalist society, (the change-over period is probably the late 1970s for most authors). Accounts vary, but the suggestion of a fundamental shift in the way the economy is structured also refers to an "information age," or a new "knowledge-based economy" as being dominant, and to the nature of work as having been transformed from being Fordist or Taylorist in nature (typified as factory assembly line jobs, and jobs that are otherwise very routine and offer few learning opportunities), to participatory, flexible, varied, knowledge-rich jobs.

The more we discuss this change, the more extensive and real it seems. But we should always ask ourselves a number of key questions: What exactly is the extent of this change? How has it impacted upon the life and work of ordinary people? Who benefits from this discourse about the change? Has ownership and control of the economy changed?

For example, it is worth reflecting on the changes that have taken place in the Canadian economy. Yes, Canada has moved from being dominantly a primary producer of agricultural products and raw materials, first to an industrial economy, and now to a predominantly service sector-economy. But the change is not as definitive as it might seem. If we look at the changes in terms of the contribution of the primary sector (agriculture, mining, fishing, etc.), the secondary sector (manufacturing and construction), and the tertiary sector (services—government, personal and financial, entertainment, etc.) to Gross Domestic Product (GDP), the major decline is within the primary sector of the economy. [The data below are from Finkel, Conrad and Strong-Boag, 1993 (Ch. 8 and 11); Wotherspoon, 2004 (Ch. 6); and from data retrieved from Statistics Canada (ww.statcan.ca) and the CIA's *World Factbook* (www.cia.gov/cia/publications/factbook).]

Agriculture, fishing and traditional mining have all declined as a proportion of GDP: Primary production is down from 26% in 1920 to about 5% today, while the secondary sector rose to about 30% by 1920 and stayed at or just below that level until 1970, and declined slightly thereafter to about 25% today. The biggest change is in the tertiary sector, which has grown from about 35% in 1920 to 61% today. (Note that these GDP statistics include a category entitled "other"; it hovers at around 10%.)

The important point is that industrial production was never dominant. Even in the key period of industrialisation, the tertiary sector was a larger contributor to GDP than was industry, and although Canada was never as industrial as some other economies, it is not so very different in this respect. Industrial activity (especially if you subtract construction) was typically no more than a third of any Western country's economic activity.

It can be argued, however, that much of the previous primary and more importantly, tertiary sector activity was geared towards the needs of industrialization, and that the tertiary sector is now generating its own needs, separate from industrial requirements. The growth of information technology is an example. Also, manufacturing employment levels have continued to decline (about 25% of the workforce worked in industry until the mid 1960s, down to about 15% today) and employment in services (not including public administration) has tripled since the Second World War (about 40% of the workforce today is now in services, and the total for all tertiary employment is about 74%) resulting in a significant change in the nature of work.

The point, however, remains—the shift is not so much from indus-trial to post-industrial as from primary production to tertiary activities. The secondary sector is still important, and the value produced within it continues to rise in real terms. We do not eat, live in, drive or wear "knowledge"—the so-called knowledge economy may affect the way all of these things are produced, but they are still produced, either in Canada or elsewhere. Also noteworthy is the stability of extraction activity—oil and gas, wood (and pulp production), mining (after allowing for the decline in coal and iron ore)—in real value terms within GDP, and the importance of these in Canadian trade (for example, half of all Canadian oil and more than three-quarters of Canadian natural gas is exported). Canada trades about 30% of its GDP. More than two-thirds of that trade is with the USA Canada is part of the global economy—it has been for a long time, exporting first furs, then wheat, then oil and gas and importing varying kinds and amounts of foodstuffs and manufacturing goods. But, the overwhelming majority of the goods and services produced in Canada are consumed in Canada (a situation similar to that in other developed economies).

What we have then is a shift in economic activity and in work. It has been described as a move from industrial to post-industrial, but this is an exaggeration: Industry is still important. What has happened is that the tertiary sector has grown faster than the other two sectors changing the balance of the economy. It should also be noted that many of the employ-ment relations associated with "post-industrialism" (within the fast-food sector, for example) are not so different from industrial work—although lower paid, often part-time, perhaps more insecure and performed by women and immigrants. See Hennessy and Sawchuck (2003) for a discus-sion of the deskilling and "industrializing" of frontline social service workers following the introduction of new technology in their jobs.

To further argue that we are now in a "post-capitalist" phase seems somewhat disingenuous, given the importance of large transnational corporations. The way corporations function may have changed and the importance of marketing and branding may be different from 20 years ago—not only for their everyday activity but also for the way they are valued on the stock exchange—but they are still "capitalist" organizations (see Klein, 2000, for a discussion of these issues). There have been plenty of reports recently on the continuing high rewards paid to CEOs, even as their companies (some of which are Canadian) perform badly. Although institutions such as insurance companies and pension funds are much more prominent as shareholders, substantial individual shareholdings continue and are highly concentrated among the wealthy. Income and personally held wealth has not changed over the last 40 years—the richest 20% of the population retain 40% of all income and the poorest 20% have just 6%. Personally held wealth (property, cars, shares, etc.) is even more highly concentrated, with the richest 20% of families owning more than 50% of total wealth. Company share ownership is more concentrated still: Two-thirds of the largest Canadian corporations were controlled by a single owner or family (Kendall, Murray and Linden, 2000, p. 255–256).

Another key question is whether the nature of work and "organizations" have changed that much for the majority of workers. Do fast-food or e-commerce employees (whether or not they are described as associates or partners) have very different and more satisfying jobs than factory workers? Is there more job security in the economy or less? Should the change in job security be described as "flexibility" or as a lack of corporate commitment to the workforce? Are the key decisions in the organization (be it public or private) taken at the top or are they shared with the workforce in some way? Who owns and controls the organization? Who gets rich from its activity (for example, the senior executives at Enron or Conrad Black at Hollinger), and is any person, society or the environment harmed in any way as a result of its activity? The texts on workplace learning are often light on the discussion of these issues, preferring to concentrate on learning at work as if there are no real issues of power and control, and as if all organizations are neutral, acting only for the benefit of all the stakeholders and society. Students should not suspend their critical understandings and their everyday experience when reading this literature.

A 2003 report by Statistics Canada (Beckstead and Gellatly, 2003) charting the changes in the Canadian economy acknowledges that not all employees in "information and communications technology industries" (ICT) and science industries are "knowledge workers," although as many as half might be classified that way. They also point out that the number of knowledge workers in other sectors (90% of the Canadian economy) has declined to about 12% (down from 17% in 1981). Only 10% of the Canadian workforce is in ICT and science sectors, and although these sectors can be presented as dynamic (with impressive employment growth in ICT), it would be safe to assume that, by Statistics Canada definitions, less than 20% of the total workforce is employed in knowledge occupations; furthermore, many of these workers are in "old" knowledge occupations (medicine, dentistry, engineering, law, etc.) rather than "new" ones (p. 35–36). Only one in eight new service jobs outside of the ICT and science areas can be described as knowledge jobs (p. 37). It is important to acknowledge that all workers have knowledge and apply it at work, but it is also important to recognize that Statistics Canada is noting something that workers have been reporting on for some time—the opportunities to apply knowledge at work is in decline; "deskilling" rather than "re-skilling" is the norm, and workers' knowledge is underemployed. While there may be specific skill shortages, Canada has, in general, a knowledgeable workforce, but not the jobs to match it (Livingstone, 1999).

Learning at Work

"Learning at work" has become a key area for adult educators. We will examine it in some detail, but first, some preparatory caveats are needed. Learning at work is not a new phenomenon, workers have always done it. Furthermore, what they have learned has always been diverse, ranging from learning about the job and how to do the work, to how to relate to fellow workers, supervisors and bosses (the social relations of work), to gaining understandings about the nature of work itself and how work affects society. Some of what workers learn is useful to the employers, some useful to workers themselves, some to their union organization at work, and some to more than one of these. Some may have little to do with work itself. It cannot be assumed that all learning at work translates into "organizational learning" and is "win-win" for workers and employers alike.

What has changed is that employers are paying more attention to the idea of workplace learning and are trying to harness such learning to meet organizational goals. This does not always result in "empowerment" for workers: In some circumstances, it may result in greater job control for workers, but in others it may result in the reverse. There is a tendency in the literature to slip from discussing workplace learning to empowerment to industrial democracy as if they are all one and the same process, and to assume, for example, that when a company states that it is empowering its workforce, it is actually doing so. Such claims always need to be tested against employee as well as employer experience.

Workers, generally speaking, have always tried to make meaning out of their work experience. It's difficult for someone to spend eight hours a day, five days a week, doing something in a totally detached way, and it's even more difficult if a person hates every minute of it. Read most accounts of workers describing their work and this becomes clear. Workers have always wanted to do a good job, even if that job is menial. The new emphasis on workplace learning should not mask that pre-existing situation.

"Our Employees Are Our Most Valuable Resource"

This phrase has become the mantra of modern corporations. What is not clear is how many companies actually believe it or act as if they really mean it. From a human resource management (HRM) perspective it places the functions of HR departments right at the centre of corporate activity and therefore writers on HRM or work and learning can perhaps be excused for not wanting to subject the statement to close scrutiny. If it is true, then HRM and human resource development (HRD) really are important. However, when companies get into trouble, they usually "downsize"; that is, the first response is often to layoff workers. The work may then be outsourced, never to return. These actions may be partially determined by market circumstances, but whatever it is that is driving company policy, whenever this happens, it should call into question the assertion that "employees are our most valuable resource."

Some organizations may well believe that the company's competitive advantage depends on a happy and committed workforce, and may work towards that end (full-time employees, higher skills, job flexibility, workplace learning), but others may equally believe that tight control of labour costs combined with close supervision over employees is the road to success (low-paid, part-time employees, routine jobs). Both approaches can work "equally well" (Bratton et. al., 2004, p. 71), being an HRD professional in the first organization may well be more satisfying than in the second.

It may be the case that the organization works hard to involve its employees—referring to them as associates or partners, developing open door policies, etc.—but it does not follow that they will be well rewarded. An article in *The Wall Street Journal* (March 26, 2004, p. B1) under the heading "Costco's Dilemma: Be Kind To Its Workers, or Wall Street," contrasts Costco's more generous salary and benefits package to Wal-Mart's "parsimonious approach to employee compensation." According to the article, some analysts and investors claim Costco's generosity to its employees is at the expense of shareholders, and that shareholders' interests should come first (in law, shareholders have no responsibility to other stakeholders). Wal-Mart is renowned for its policy of driving down supplier costs, regardless of the impact on the workers in less-developed countries who are making the products for its stores in North America. Its aggressive marketing (big box stores), low wage policies, and anti-unionism have met opposition in North America, but its shareholders are happy, earnings per share are significantly higher than at Costco. HR professionals work in both companies.

Human Capital Theory

The contribution of education and training to overall economic development and growth, as well as to an individual's economic future, has been recognized for some time. The discussion of the Mechanics' Institute in Chapter 1 serves as an illustration of this point. However, the idea that education could be an important contributor to economic growth, and therefore, a main purpose of education should be to support economy, was established in the late 1950s and early 1960s. It was during this period of "full employment" in the main Western economies that attention turned to increasing the productivity of existing labour through training and retraining and by more targeted education of existing and future labour. It was argued that education could be divided into "investment" and "consumption" activities and that state funds should primarily support investment in "human capital."

The skills and knowledge that working people gained through education and training, by formal, non-formal and informal learning activities, were likened to a form of "capital" resulting from deliberate investments. These investments in human capital were held to be the major reason for the faster, more developed state of modern economies (Schultz, 1961). What followed from this argument was a view that countries should control the expansion and the mix of their education system in order to maximize economic growth. This human capital theory had clear implications for schools and the formal higher education system as well as for adult education in general. It pushed all of them to justify their educational activity in economic terms, as opposed to liberal educational ones.

Not only were the relative costs of different education programs examined, but arguments were made as to the rate-of-return that a particular education course (an investment) could expect to yield and what investments (education) should be made to fulfill "manpower forecasts." The argument that labour was a form of human capital, that economic development hinged on these investments, and that education should be in the service of economy, essentially in the service of capitalist production, was hotly debated (Shaffer, 1961). However, human capital theory has remained as an important starting point for many of the current arguments in adult education literature debating workplace learning/education. For example, Mechthild Hart observes that there are two dominant approaches:

> The first...the skills approach, emphasizes the skill requirements of the future workforce in light of the need of corporate America to stay competitive in the world market and looks at work and workers from the perspective of "human capital" (Hart, 1995, p. 20).

While some of these arguments for a skills approach may be rooted in an understanding of rapid technological and economic change, they are traditional in their concern of education and training of workers as human capital (Welton, 1991).

The second approach sees workplace learning as developmental and cultural but even here the major contributions (Marsick, 1987, 1988; and Marsick and Watkins, 1990), according to Hart,

> Operate within a framework of conventional, status-quo-orientated assumptions about current social and economic arrangements, and owe their legitimatory framework entirely to human capital theory (1995, p. 20).

The more critical contributions to these debates offered by Welton (1991) and Hart (1992), among others, see workplace learning in a broader framework, interacting with other adult educational and learning activity (see Foley, 1995, for a more comprehensive list of authors engaged in this debate). But nonetheless, it could be claimed that they divorce the education of workers from "the lives and struggles of working people" (Foley, 1995, p. 122). To the extent that they do this, they sidestep the political economy of work and workplace relations by accepting a post-Fordist, post-capitalist, post-modern (see Harvey, 1989, for a more elaborate discussion of these terms) explanation of economy and society, which masks questions of economic power, ownership and control. Therefore, it can be argued that their view of workplace learning, as it applies in the workplace, also accepts the precepts of human capital theory. However, the purpose of Hart's (1992) analysis is to argue for an education for life and to "criticize the distortions and limitations of predominant views on work and education" (p. 214).

Worker Education and Training

The current emphasis on creating a "leaner" state, one less concerned with the provision of a range of social services and essentially working more narrowly to attract investment from global capital, has led to governments shedding "personal interest and development" and "social action and social change" adult education and, instead, concentrating their resources on "academic, credential and vocational" education for adults (to use the three categories of Selman et al., p. 410). This funded support for vocationally relevant adult education illustrates very clearly that the dominant state view of the purpose of adult education is that it should support the economy. Today, fewer adult educators are working in non-formal educational settings, in community based programs, or in liberal adult education, and more are involved in vocational training.

This trend towards withdrawal of public funds from courses that are not geared towards training, retraining and general vocational credentials can be seen across Canada. As resources are cut, questions are asked about the relevance of liberal arts to a career, or the economic value of a particular community education program. Increasingly, traditional non-vocational courses have been forced to become partially or wholly self-financing; new courses have to be justified in terms of their economic benefits if they are to receive public funds.

This emphasis on improving a country's human capital has led to demands for a national vocational qualifications scheme. Such schemes are more advanced outside of Canada, with both Australia and Britain providing examples of recently developed schemes, and are specifically designed to enhance the skill levels of workers and to support a move towards higher skilled, knowledge-based employment. While there is little hard evidence to suggest that such schemes will succeed in meeting their broad economic goals, they do illustrate the extent of state involvement in establishing a worker education and training model for adult education.

The schemes may also have a number of benefits for workers:

- previously ignored skills become recognized;
- workers may move vertically through some skill groupings regardless of late entry into the workforce or lack of formal apprenticeship training;
- a national scheme may free some workers from the restrictions of employer-specific training and allow them to move between jobs;
- schemes may include an acknowledgment of prior learning and transferability of credentials — see Martin (Chapter 12) and Thomas (Chapter 26) in *Learning for Life* and the discussions on training, particularly Chapter 3 on Quebec, in *The Foundations of Adult Education in Canada*.

While these developments can be regarded as generally beneficial, because along with the growth of investment in the nation's human capital working people also benefit, this emphasis can result in a narrowing of adult education purpose to serve existing economic interests. The emphasis on training may also mask the way politicians use training and retraining to cut welfare and keep the unemployed "occupied" within a "training industry"—constantly upgrading skills but never achieving permanent skilled work (Swift, 1995; Duffy et al., 1997).

As a complement to these developments, training and educational objectives are increasingly being expressed in terms of the "competencies" to be achieved. Particular skills have been broken down into a series of incremental competencies. In competence-based training programs, trainees only move on to the next level of training when they have achieved the competencies identified. There has also been some criticism of this approach:

- compartmentalization and fragmentation of knowledge occurs (Collins, 1991); and
- there are practical limitations of breaking down all skills into detailed subsets of skill prerequisites.

In spite of these limitations, competence-based programs are being extended to include communication, collective (for example, working in groups) and representational (representing fellow workers) skills as well as motor skills. These kinds of changes, together with a looser definition of competencies (sometimes expressed as "learning outcomes") and the necessary prerequisites of any particular skill or educational achievement, may save this concept from impracticality, but it remains a limited educational approach. It favours training over education and the acquisition of particular skills and knowledge over a critical, liberal adult education. (See Chapter 25 by Peruniak in *Learning for Life* for a fuller discussion.)

Human-Resource Management

As indicated earlier in the discussion about the pervasiveness of human capital theory, there has been a growth in literature on workplace learning in the context of new human-resource management (HRM) techniques. This area of scholarship has drawn commentary from diverse fields including management, labour relations, politics and social science as well as education.

Students should be aware, however, that HRM as a field of study has attracted some criticism. It might generally be agreed that employers need a human-resource management policy to ensure consistent treatment of employees and that a human-resource management function can help employers observe basic employment equity and health and safety legislation. However, some critics argue that these HRM functions are too often used to enforce management rights over employees and, at best, ensure only minimum compliance with statutes. A more severe criticism may relate to the company products (for example, cigarettes) or use of natural resources (for example, clear-cutting forestry) and argue that all HRM does is ensure workers' compliance in these "harmful" company activities.

The recent development of HRM into a central plank of company policy—designed to give companies the "cutting edge" vis-à-vis the competition by involving workers more in company activity—has heightened this criticism. HRM has always been concerned with maximizing the output from employees and recent attempts to involve workers more in some aspects of company decision-making is designed ultimately to maximize company output and profit. This application of HRM is based on the belief that employers and employees have similar interests and goals. New HRM is, therefore, based on a "unitary" theory of labour relations. It denies that there might be divergent interests between those of the employer and employee or that employees in one company might have common interests (some would say "class" interests) with workers in other companies. Some would argue that HRM is only necessary because labour (human resources) has been separated from owning and controlling the productive process and, therefore, needs to be managed (Ellerman, 1990).

The fact that many companies recognize labour unions and that HRM specialists are involved in formulating and administering labour contract agreements does not undermine this critique. In fact, it underscores the point. In negotiations, the function of the HRM department is to support the management negotiators and, after completion of the agreement, HRM will try to ensure worker and union compliance with the contract and work to prevent any further encroachment on management rights. It is in this context that the expressed desires of companies to involve and empower workers through new human-resource strategies should be considered.

Organizational Culture and Workplace Learning

As noted earlier, workers learn at work all the time and always have. They learn about a lot of things: how to do the job, how to relate to other workers and supervisors and how their work affects society. If there is a union, they may learn about the union and how it operates. If there is no union, they may well learn why unions are considered beneficial by some. They learn about power and authority. They are encouraged to learn about what is useful for the employer. They learn about how their interests overlap with those of the employer, and about times when they do not. It is clear that some of their learning may contribute to a "culture of silence," to an acceptance of the way things are. Workers may learn to accept the dominant ideology that supports management rights; for example, the idea that we are all part of a global economy and must strive to out-compete others in order to survive. Workplace learning is not new: What is new is the emphasis now placed on it, and the belief that real workplace learning is that which enriches the employer, whether or not it enriches the worker. Other workplace learning—for example, some of the kinds of learning listed above—does not count.

To ignore power and authority is to ignore the realities of what it is to be an employee. The relationship between culture and the underlying system of production is obvious, although complex. Managerially determined organizational culture is not ordinary—it is imposed. Edgar Schein, Professor at the MIT Sloan School of Management defines organizational culture as:

> The pattern of basic assumptions that a given group has invented, discovered, or developed in learning to cope with its problems of external adaptation and internal integration, and that have worked well enough to be considered valid, and, therefore, to be taught to new members as the correct way to perceive, think, and feel in relation to those problems (1985, p. 12).

Not all definitions of organizational culture will be as clearly stated in relation to managerial power as that of Schein's—he notes that assumptions have to be "valid" and a "correct way to perceive, think, and feel" —but it is clear in practice that organizational culture is something to be determined and molded by management. For most employees, organizational culture is what management says it is. Employees are expected "to be on the same page," to accept the mission statement of the organization, and to "buy into" the organizational goals. Organizational culture is that which is determined by management, and learning about that culture is learning to accept it.

John Storey, a leading business school professor in the United Kingdom, has commented that the "management of culture" has become a distinguishing feature of HRM, and dates the "remarkable trend" away from "personnel procedures and rules" to the "management of culture" to the early- to mid-1990s (Storey, 2001, p. 8). He comments that "managing cultural change and moving towards HRM can often appear to coincide and become one and the same project." Corporate cultural management is "perceived to offer the key to the unlocking of consensus, flexibility and commitment."

The idea behind this shift is clear: consensus would displace conflict (and collective bargaining), flexibility (a "substitute term for greater management control" [p. 8]) would increase productivity, and commitment would lift labour performance higher—"committed employees would 'go the extra mile' in pursuit of customer service and organizational goals" (p. 8). To achieve all of this means changing a whole set of workers' behaviours, attitudes and values, displacing workers' culture (no matter how contradictory that culture may be) and imposing that of management. In process, a "pluralist" (with different interests that sometimes coincide and sometimes conflict) and quasi democratic culture (with unions challenging management decisions in collective bargaining) is displaced by a "unitarist" (with everyone in the organization assumed to be sharing exactly the same goals) and a pretend democratic culture (with claims of empowerment and teams).

Workplace Change and Workplace Learning

There has been a continual stream of schemes claiming to increase job satisfaction for workers and cut company costs. What drives this is the realization that in traditional companies employers are not very interested in what workers think and that many employees have little control over how they spend their time at work. Therefore, it is argued, workers feel alienated from their work and, if employers want employee loyalty, they must improve the quality of working life (QWL) for their employees. Another driving force is the perceived need to meet the competitive challenge, to match Japanese management techniques, and generally to cut waste. This argument leads to just-in-time (JIT) stock control, team production techniques and total quality management (TQM). Some might argue that regardless of the origins of these new methods, current HRM techniques are much more humanistic and that work in most modern industries is fulfilling, certainly more so than in previous times. While this might be true for some workers, particularly those in professional or skilled occupations, it is not the case for all of them. Some new job areas, particularly in the service industries, do not demand such high standards for their employees.

This renewed focus on human resources is helping to redefine human-resource management as central to organizational success. The initial concerns of manufacturing companies have spread to service companies and public sector organizations. Consultants abound spreading this new gospel—managers are redefined as leaders and coaches, workers as associates or members, and factories and offices as "learning organizations." This revived version of human capital theory emphasizes the competitive edge to be gained from a committed skilled workforce, one that is learning to tackle company problems in new ways.

Some of the writing in this area stems from a belief that we are now living in a post-bureaucracy, post-Fordist, post-industrial, post-modern, even post-capitalist society and that Fordist mass-production techniques, based on Frederick Taylor's "scientific management" approach to work organization, are no longer appropriate. For some authors, adversarial union attitudes are also seen as inappropriate in this perceived new climate. "Toyotarist" production methods (teams, company unions, JIT, TQM), which claim that decisions are based locally in "cells," are sometimes contrasted with the alienation associated with machine-paced assembly lines. Toyotarist production is depicted as collaborative. As such, claims are made that production is more differentiated than it was previously; companies compete more on quality than price and, therefore, employees must be empowered to produce quality goods and services.

Although there has been a shift away from mass production techniques in industry and an extension of service employment together with a move towards smaller production units, many of the jobs in both services and industry remain repetitive, largely unchallenging, and low paid. For example, jobs in fast-food outlets, often referred to as "McJobs," are low skilled, low paid and part-time. This shift to post-industrial society and towards new participatory management styles is, therefore, overstated.

Many of the accounts recording the successes to be gained by implementing new HRM are written by management consultants who have a vested interest in its continuance. Supporters of this new management style emphasize

- greater worker control over the design of jobs;
- more worker contributions to the functioning of the organization;
- reduced absenteeism; and
- major cost savings.

However, some companies have had to amend their initial enthusiasm as economic conditions have worsened, with workers being laid off and TQM abandoned. Some companies that have adopted these new human-resource strategies and have operated with them for some time have still reached bankruptcy in recent recessions (*Newsweek*, 1992). Nortel, the leading information technology company in Canada, has repeatedly decreased its workforce since the beginning of 2000.

Some of the more careful research has shown mixed results from adopting QWL, team concept and other methods. In some cases, workers who accepted greater responsibilities did not gain more control over their time and work (Klein, 1989). In other cases, workers enjoyed some job rotation but generally did not believe they were gaining new skills. Although management did listen to workers' suggestions, these often resulted in job intensification and speed-ups (Robertson, 1989).

One study concluded that the market conditions and methods of production were crucial to the success of new managerial practices. Companies that enjoyed a market niche and batch-production methods using skilled workers fared better than those competing in a more competitive mass-production market. Under the right conditions, there could be enhanced job security, skills and employee satisfaction; but for other less-skilled workers, there could also be job losses, speed-ups and dissatisfaction (Bratton, 1992).

Clearly, organizations that adopt these new techniques are seeking to enlist workers' knowledge, ingenuity and cooperation to cut waste and compete more successfully. Some are also hoping to turn workers away from unionization and to bind workers to company objectives. Although workers can gain greater job satisfaction, in the right conditions, from some of these human-resource management policies, it is an exaggeration to describe all of these as simply "win-win" situations in which workers gain as much as employers.

Much of the literature celebrating these new methods describes these policies as creating a "sense of shared ownership" and control of the enterprise (Senge, 1990, p. 13) and claim a "sense of job ownership" (Wellins, 1991, pp. 10–11) among employees. This, however, is not the same thing as workers actually owning and controlling. Perhaps this is why management guru, Peter Senge, also emphasizes that the role of the "leader"—that is manager—is to "help people restructure their views of reality." While these "learning organizations" (companies) are often contrasted with "traditional" companies, they are rarely compared to actual worker-owned enterprises in which worker job control and empowerment might be considered more complete (see the Mondragon co-operative case study which follows).

From Factory to Knowledge Work

The shift from a Taylorist/Fordist workplace to a knowledge/teams workplace has been argued repeatedly, the contention being that work on the mind-numbing conveyor belt has been replaced by creative teams striving for ever greater customer satisfaction according to these accounts (Boreham, 2002). This change is often exaggerated: Factory conditions still exist (if not so much in developed countries, then certainly in the outsourced plants located in less economically developed ones), and new fast-food and retail jobs are low paid, part time and insecure. As noted earlier, knowledge jobs are few and can also be insecure. Hiding within "knowledge companies" are many boring, routine jobs. There may be a steady demand for very well-qualified individuals, but the greatest growth is in low-paid, casual and part-time labour (Lowe, 2000). It may be the case that a greater attempt has been made to involve many workers in low-level company decisions, in problem solving and in customer service, but whether or not this effort deserves to be called empowering is at best a moot point—it could equally be described as limiting if not as co-opting.

Although more astute researchers have argued that Taylorist measurement and control at work remains or has been expanded (for example, Hennessy and Sawchuk, 2003)—Taylorism may have changed in form but its essential purpose has not—the assertion that change *has* taken place persists. As Tony Brown comments:

> Most descriptions contrast team production to the "scientific management" principles of Taylor. In fact the tendency is in the other direction—to specify every move that a worker makes in much greater detail than before. Management chooses the processes, basic production layout and technologies to be used. Speeding up the pace of work is an intended consequence of standardising production, services or software (Brown, 1999, p. 15).

All of this is made possible by applying new technology into the "new workplace." The largest numbers of jobs are now found in the service sector and, within that sector, many jobs can be described as white collar and as linked to new technology. Some jobs are being dispersed into the home ("teleworkers"), and are not required to be completed at a particular time or in a specifically designated, employer-owned space. The appearance of worker control over when and how much work is undertaken is illusionary, however, because the new computer-based work comes with constant monitoring and feedback to the employer—far exceeding what Taylor was able to do with his stopwatch and clipboard. What we have today could perhaps be described as a more differentiated or "post-modern Taylorism."

Alongside this shift in perception of employment relations has been a new emphasis on the importance of work-based learning; the term *workplace learning* has been developed to mean all that is *good* about learning at work. According to this perspective, workers develop and learn, and the organization learns. It has been argued that the knowledge required to successfully engage at work has changed from simple know-how to "work process knowledge"—knowledge that "links know-how to theory," a kind of knowledge that was not available in the traditional Taylorist workplace (Boreham, 2002). Exactly what this theory to be learned is remains unclear. Furthermore, it is unconvincing to argue that workers did not previously possess something akin to work process knowledge (assuming that we can agree on a definition and on its existence—let us assume it implies an understanding of the production process beyond a particular worker's own job), although it might be the case that few of them ever got to apply it. But is the real purpose of "work process knowledge" to turn workers away from understandings of ownership, authority and control, and towards accepting managerial objectives and employer ownership of value added in the production process?

Learning Organizations

With all the rhetoric surrounding new workplace organization, the knowledge economy, and the claim that we live in a post-industrial, even post-capitalist, global economy, it is easy to forget that the basic structure and purpose of large corporations has not changed. Once we acknowledge that there are different interpretations of workplace learning, and that organizations are not unitary but pluralist in nature, we can begin to examine different interests and outcomes. We live in societies (some would argue in one global society) in which the gap between the richest and the poorest, between those who live full lives in the economically developed countries and those who live "half lives at best" in the less developed countries, is growing (Honderich, 2002, p. 6). Many workers in the developed countries have experienced a decline in the value of real wages, and they must struggle to stay abreast of inflation even at low inflation rates, while the incomes of the rich continue to climb. The following quote is from *Macleans* magazine, a proponent of free enterprise:

> From 1970 to 1999, the average annual salary in the U.S. rose roughly 10 per cent to US$35,864, says Paul Krugman, a professor at Princeton University. At the same time, the average pay package of *Fortune* magazine's top 100 CEOs was up an astonishing 2,785 per cent, to US$37.5 million. "There is no rationale but avarice and greed," says (John) Crispo. "I believe in the pursuit of self-interest, but look at what they do: they rob us blind" (2002).

John Crispo is a retired University of Toronto business professor and outspoken champion of corporate freedom and free trade, who has long been associated with the right wing think tank—the Howe Institute.

As noted earlier, being a worker in a learning organization is not a guarantee of job security. It may be true that the company's competitive position depends on a more effective and intelligent use of its human resources, but this does not mean that a corporate decision about location or product development will benefit a particular workgroup, or that the rewards from the collective effort will be equitably distributed amongst the workforce. Employees can lose even in cases where they are given a small stake in the company; in the Enron case, employee shareholdings were locked in and became worthless, while the senior executives bailed, taking their inflated funds with them. The decision to close a work site, for example, may have absolutely nothing to do with how that particular workforce has performed; or how committed they were to the learning organization.

Laurie Field (2004), a proponent of organizational learning for ten years, has rethought his commitment to the idea. He considers that the weakness in the conception of organizational learning stems first from a confusing and ambiguous use of the terms "organization" and "learning"; second from the focus on "learning associated with technical and economic interests"; and third from the assumption that organizations are unitary (p. 204–205). He concludes:

> Whole organisations rarely learn. A great deal of what has been referred to in the literature as 'organisational learning' is actually learning by shared-interest groups within organizations (p. 216).

The Pedagogics of Work and Learning

In September 1999, the *First International Conference on Researching Work and Learning* was held at Leeds University, England. It was hosted by the School of Continuing Education, where more than 20 years of research has been conducted with and by working people into the conditions of work, unemployment and the relationship between work and community. Much of the Leeds' work had been conducted directly with labour unions and union members at the workplace. Given this context, it is somewhat surprising to hear Keith Forrester, the leading Leeds researcher admit:

> We too have not attached sufficient weight to the inter-relationship between employee learning, new management practices and the wider 'modernising' strategies currently being pursued by New Labour in this country, and to a lesser extent, in a number of other countries (Forrester, 1999, p. 188).

If they missed it at Leeds—with its focus on workers' interests—it is perhaps more understandable to consider how it has been overlooked more generally in the workplace learning literature, much of which claims either a neutral position or assumes a more overtly managerial perspective. The enthusiasm for lifelong learning, the learning society, and learning organizations has dulled researchers' critical gaze as to what exactly is going on in workplace learning.

Forrester defines the problem in the following terms:

> In the increased competitive pressure on management to improve the quality and quantity of the labour input, the notion of employee subjectivity (affective elements such as initiative, 'emotional labour' [customer care], values and attitudes, intra-individual management, self actualisation and adaptability) has emerged as a key area of new management and thinking and that workplace or work-related learning is often seen as an essential part of 'capturing' employee subjectivity in achieving corporate objectives. The wider socio-economic changes of recent decades has resulted in many workplaces questioning aspects of the traditionalist 'Taylorist' division between thinking and doing along with the rigidities characteristic of a Fordist workplace regime. *However, instead of the brave new world of employee 'empowerment', 'autonomy', satisfaction and fulfilment within those 'new workplaces' or 'workplaces of the future' there is just as likely, we suggest, to emerge new mechanisms of oppression and managerial control. If this is the case, or at least a possibility, then there is the danger that the equally brave new world of peda-*

gogics in relation to 'work and learning' will become part of the new forms of oppression and control in the workplace (Forrester, 1999, p. 188. Emphasis added.)

In order to evaluate this insight, we need to reflect on our previous discussion of workplace learning and its genesis in new human-resource management and human capital theory. Forrester's observation is supported by a study of skills-training policies in Australia and Aotearoa/New Zealand, which also draws on UK and Canadian literature. The authors comment on how a consensus is promoted on the assumption of a unitarist mutual benefit approach. "Yet the resulting reforms have had a remarkably unilateral effect: they move control over and benefits from skill training away from individuals and unions and into the hands of private capital" (Jackson and Jordan, 2000, p. 195).

Two texts, one Canadian the other from the US, have attempted to map out what is needed if we are to see public policy supporting genuine worker empowerment. Graham Lowe's (2000) *The Quality of Work: A People-Centred Agenda* and Joe Kincheloe's (1999) *How Do We Tell the Workers? The Socioeconomic Foundations of Work and Vocational Education* are very different approaches to resolving the same problem: how to achieve *good work*—high quality jobs along with enhanced democracy at work and in society.

Lowe's study draws on years of surveying the opinions of Canadians on social and economic issues. He found a deep dissatisfaction with work, with not only the insecurity of employment in the 1990s, but also with the nature of work itself. Employees consistently report that, for the jobs they perform, they are overqualified, and their skills and knowledge are underemployed. High technology and knowledge jobs are scarce, while mundane, repetitive, low-paid jobs are commonplace. The study is supplemented by case study data that illustrate workers' experience in the modern workplace. Lowe also argues for a balance between work and non-work.

Kincheloe's text is twice the length of Lowe's; it is a denser argument, drawing on diverse sources to support his analysis. He approaches the issues as an educator interested in how we should teach about the world of work (what he calls vocational education). He addresses questions of diversity and the nature of government, all with a view to contesting the free market claims of corporate America and recapturing what he sees as humane and democratic traditions of US society. He believes the democratic future of the US depends upon the democratizing of the work world.

Both researchers demonstrate a good understanding of the contextual issues: For example, they do not reify the learning organization model, they point to examples of bad practice, of the rhetoric of learning organizations not matching workers' reality. They understand the limitations of corporate self-interest and acknowledge that an active, interventionist and regulatory role for government can be a positive force. They have a healthy respect for labour unions and advocate (without preaching) a role for unions within the process. However, they both believe that employers can change and will benefit from democratic change. It is refreshing to read two accounts of work and learning that acknowledge that inequalities of power exist even if they do sometimes suspend this understanding in their enthusiasm for advocating collaboration and change.

Neither author really deals adequately with one of the central contradictions of modern corporations. Corporate allegiance to the primacy of shareholder and CEO interests (bolstered by the legal framework), and to the central purpose of increasing profit margins (bolstered by dubious economic theory), relegates the concerns and needs of other stakeholders to minority roles. The central contradiction of private enterprise remains—large corporations create hierarchies of control and power and are driven by the profit motive. These control, power and profit relations create the social relations within work and society—those of employer and employee, boss and worker. Society's social classes result from these dominant work relations, in fact, it can be argued that with the shrinkage of well-paid manual and office jobs—described as the "middle class" in North America—is in retreat and society is polarizing into a large working class and a relatively small elite. A veil may be drawn over these contradictions at times with the rhetoric of workers as associates or partners but unless ownership and control changes and becomes genuinely more equitably distributed, fundamentally nothing has changed.

Lowe and Kincheloe do shift the focus of workplace learning researchers away from the narrow gaze on isolated workplace change and establish the importance of understanding the large-scale breadth and depth of change needed in work and societal relations if any meaningful large-scale change is to occur. The authors establish the need for scholars to grasp the multi/inter/cross-disciplinary nature of the problem under investigation. Can North America change the way business is done? Unfortunately, the federal/provincial divide in Canadian politics makes it very difficult to establish a common political environment, even if there was a desire to contest the neo-liberal economic agenda (deregulation, privatization, open global markets, minimal government) and the US shows no signs of adopting a Kincheloe view of the role of government. Also there is not much evidence of change in corporate behaviour. Joel Bakan's *The Corporation: The Pathological Pursuit of Power* (2002) provides a damning condemnation of corporate behaviour rooted in corporate law and structures. His radical reform agenda has not found any champions within governments in North America. Bratton et al. (2004) is one of the few texts to provide a critical overview of workplace learning.

Educators, particularly adult educators, have embraced the notion of the workplace as a site for learning. In many cases, they have offered their services as consultants, describing themselves as human resource development specialists. They have searched out examples of good practice, describing it as "development work" (Welton, 1991), "empowerment" and a long-overdue recognition of the skills and knowledge that workers possess. In some cases, acting in consort with consultants from other disciplinary backgrounds, they have extolled the virtues of "team concept," "kaizen" and the learning organization in general (for a critical discussion of learning organizations see Fenwick, 1998). They have accepted competency-based or outcome-based training as the norm, and have welcomed employer-determined curriculum into colleges (for critique see Peruniak, 1998). Lifelong learning is largely seen unproblematically as benefiting workers and employers, as if they had a seamless identity, as if their interests are always one and the same. While perhaps arguing for a more liberal and critical approach (after all, it is argued that many CEOs have a Bachelor of Arts degree first, and that organizations are interested in a well-educated, critical-thinking workforce [Lowe, 2000], many educators, nonetheless, abandon any serious critical reflection in service to their new masters. As Forrester was quoted earlier: "then there is the danger that the equally brave new world of pedagogics in relation to 'work and learning' will become part of the new forms of oppression and control in the workplace." Unfortunately the warning can go unheeded in the adult educators' desire to be relevant and to present workplace learning as a separate entity equally beneficial to all. Many writers acknowledge different interests but reduce workplace learning to a list of knowledge issues to be resolved and in the process treat it as a neutral, value-free activity with the hope that "perhaps somewhere can be struck a balance between employees' and employers' interests in creating the goals of workplace learning" (Fenwick, 2006).

Another problem in the literature is the tendency to treat all organizations as the same. This partly reflects the imposition of business rhetoric on non-business organizations, such as public services, universities, hospitals, non-profit and non-governmental organizations; all are seen as dealing with "clients" or "customers" within the context of a "business plan" and having to apply business principles to the "bottom line." Scant regard is paid to the notion of the public good or the quasi-democratic structures that govern these organizations and distinguish them from corporate capital.

As you read more about workplace learning, keep in mind the previous research results. A declaration that a company is seeking to establish a learning environment and to empower workers does not necessarily mean that workers will enjoy a more culturally enriched and educationally developed work experience. Management rhetoric is not necessarily reality for workers. A sausage factory might well be described in glowing terms as a "learning organization," with workers voluntarily giving up their spare time to work collectively and learn how to solve company problems together, but the story may be related from a management consultant's perspective. In an extreme case, the closure of the plant and the resulting unemployment of the workers may not even be recorded. (For a review of some of the arguments, see Chapter 11 by Fenwick in *Learning for Life*.)

Another major gap in the contemporary literature on work and education is a discussion of co-operative organization, the Mondragon system of worker-owned co-operatives is described at length in the next section of the book. These co-operatives are more successful than those of the Anti-gonish Movement and represent a contemporary example of co-operation existing alongside competition. Because this is a little-known example, it will be discussed at length prior to getting to the crux of the debate, which is (1) Are co-operatives an alternative to private "re-engineered" companies? and (2) Is the "learning" in a co-operative more developmental and democratic than in a privately "re-engineered" company?

Workers Co-operatives: The Example of Mondragon

In Canada and the United States, there have always been a number of successful worker and producer co-operatives. However, the localized and restricted success of co-operatives in Canada has dampened enthusiasm for co-operative solutions to unemployment and production problems (a residue of support exists in the Atlantic provinces and Quebec). Many co-operatives exist within a very specific set of circumstances, such as a worker buyout or within limited market and capital constraints. In Italy, however, there are some big worker-managed enterprises; in France, as well, an extensive network of co-operatives is flourishing. Even in Britain, the number of worker- and community-owned co-operatives is growing, with at least 1,500 currently operating. The Great Western Brewery in Saskatoon was bought by workers when Molsons pulled out and Algoma steel, the largest union/worker "buy-out," was formed after its US owners withdrew. See Quarter (1995) for a comprehensive review.

But perhaps the best-known and most interesting example of an alternative "mini-economy" is the Mondragon co-operatives in the Basque region of Spain. Much has been written about them and they do provide an instructive model. They are not perfect, and some would argue not even proper co-operatives, because of the form of representative democracy used to manage the companies. Nevertheless, the Mondragon co-operatives are a working model of a mini-economy founded on workers' ownership, a form of ownership that excludes capitalists. It is, therefore, an example of how workers' control of production might work in practice within a market economy, as well as an example of how larger worker-owned companies can be managed.

The Origins—Creating Jobs

The Mondragon co-operatives began with the objective of providing work in a depressed area. Their structures developed as they grew (during 1965–75, one thousand jobs a year were created). The enterprises were organized around a structure based on the workers possessing a capital stake in the co-operative. This stake was paid when entering a job and withdrawn when leaving a job. This meant that only existing workers could be owners, and yet the numbers of employed could expand. Newcomers "bought in" to specific enterprises with a small capital stake. This overcame the problem of co-operatives being limited to founding co-operators.

In the Mondragon network, the bank (which was set up three years after the first co-operative and was controlled by the co-operatives), together with its financial and coordinating functions, has come to play a pivotal role. These institutions provide finance and coordination between co-operatives and give support services to any would-be co-operative enterprise, as well as those in financial difficulties. Although crucial, they are recognized as secondary to the needs of production and are, therefore, established as a secondary co-operative with bank and financial employees and representatives from the producer co-operatives on their governing boards. (The bank was successful in mobilizing workers' savings in much the same way as the early credit unions in Canada.)

By 1989, the co-operatives had created and run their own schools, technical college, university (claiming a total of 45 educational co-operatives), housing sector (10 co-operatives), social security system and shops. All have been built on a small foundation of manufacturing production involving a total of approximately 21,000 workers.

The success of the linked enterprises supports a number of key points:

- workers can run industry without capitalists;
- there is ample surplus for societal needs in present-day production techniques (in addition to the social provision outlined, 10 percent of profits go into a social fund); and
- there are resources remaining for job creation and retention, and for research and development.

Mondragon, though small scale, also illustrates a number of other interesting features and tendencies. For example, the state, or more accurately the local state, can in some respects "wither away" (in relation to its provision of housing, schools, and social security, all of which were taken over by the co-operatives), as new forms of social relations are established.

Running the Co-operatives

Not everyone participates directly in the process of decision making within the co-operatives; there is representation rather than direct democracy, and inevitably key influence is wielded by management (similar tendencies have been shown in many studies of co-operatives in the former Yugoslavia and elsewhere). However, management is hired and fired by workers and is treated as part of the workforce, with its pay determined in a similar way to other worker–members. There are wage differentials, but these are fixed so that no manager–members are able to award themselves bonuses of more than a fixed proportion of the lowest wage. Also, all workers receive proportional capital benefits that are considerable and are enjoyed at retirement. Managers tend to be recruited from the local community and are committed to the co-operatives.

There is increased job security in the co-operatives. No firm is taken over (or moved to Mexico!) without workers' knowledge. No worker can be sacked on a whim of management. Any decision to close (or sell) an enterprise has to be agreed by a general assembly of members and approved by representatives of the other Mondragon co-operatives. Although there has been some redundancies and closures because of market failure, the linked structure of the co-operatives allowed workers to find new work in a different co-operative enterprise.

Observers have noted a distinction between the democratized forms of governance in Mondragon and more traditional in-work processes within the Mondragon companies. It has been argued that more problem-solving and democratic production processes are needed at a local level in Mondragon to overcome the tendency towards hierarchical problem solving (Greenwood and Santos, 1992).

The Co-operatives During Recession

If all the Mondragon co-operatives failed together it would be disastrous. At one time, their concentration on domestic consumer products ("white goods") did make them vulnerable. However, more recently, the bank and its offshoot operations act as "minder" of the new and troubled co-operatives. This eliminates unnecessary competition between co-operatives in the group and has stimulated diversification of Mondragon production beyond domestic products. It cannot, of course, isolate the co-operatives from the national or world economy. Recent studies suggest that the entry of Spain into the European Union and the globalization of transnational competitors are presenting problems, because Mondragon co-operatives are having to operate in more competitive markets against exploiters of cheap labour.

The following illustrates this vulnerability to the external economy:

- Mondragon jobs grew even at the outset of the mid-1970s recession, but this growth was checked in the early 1980s, with jobs remaining static (although this should be compared with a 20 percent loss in other jobs in the Basque region 1975–83).

- From 1985 to 1989, a 17 percent growth in co-operative jobs was reported, but the early 1990s has seen zero growth as the co-ops consolidate.
- there has been a growth in "temporary" non-member jobs.

Furthermore, there was a growth in temporary non-member jobs. Rapid expansion saw the number of jobs created rise from 25,000 in 1992 to 70,884 by the end of 2004, of which 49 percent were based in the Basque Country, 39 percent in the rest of Spain and 12 percent internationally. However, the majority of the new employees were not co-operative members; many of the new jobs were in distribution, and were either part-time or temporary positions. The growth in temporary jobs is a worrying trend that could undermine the co-operative ideal. While it is clearly an attempt by the co-operatives to match the cost-cutting tactics of traditional competitors, it strikes at the heart of the worker–ownership and employment-creating principles that underpin Mondragon. The co-operatives are struggling with this problem as they reorganize themselves under hostile market conditions. The May 2003 General Assembly of all Mondragon co-operatives approved a resolution regarding "membership expansion," which urged the non-co-operative "spin-off" companies to develop formulas which would enable non-member employees to partici-pate in the ownership and management of their companies (Phillips, 1991; Mondragon, n.d.; Whyte, 1999).

Paul Phillips (1991) has reported on a number of changes that the Mondragon co-operatives have made in order to adjust to changing market conditions:

- joint ventures with traditional firms;
- internal restructuring to match capitalist corporate competitors (stronger sectoral groupings); and
- a growth in the size of co-operatives through mergers.

Seeking external finance and the growth of temporary employees could now be added to Phillips's list (see Moye, 1993). All of these developments threaten co-operative independence and, as Phillips emphasized, result in more remote decision making.

At one level, these problems illustrate that co-operative forms are more compatible with a "planned" economy, or at least government interven-tion (controls to safeguard co-operative forms of ownership and regulated trade), than with unfettered markets and free trade.

The Lessons from Mondragon

How big can such a network grow? Has Mondragon reached its limit? Can it be emulated today? These are open questions. But what this small-scale operation (surely no longer an experiment) does show is that, for produc-

tion needs, planning can be undertaken through worker-controlled organizations; in this case, the secondary co-operative banking functions. What
Mondragon also shows us is that production planning does not have to
be bureaucratic or "top-down"; worker–ownership, planning and market
choice can operate constructively and harmoniously, under most conditions.

It is important to note that, although the present development of the
co-operatives is managed from the centre, the structure was built from the
"bottom up." This challenges the idea that workers' control is unable to
serve societal needs. Even if, for example, environmental concerns or the
interests of minorities were not directly addressed in the first instance, it
can be argued that, since the workers live and work in the area and are part
of the community, ignoring those needs will eventually directly reflect on
them. It is not a remote government or an absentee employer/shareholder
who is making the decisions about the nature of work in the locality, but
the workers themselves—although currently influenced by hostile market
conditions.

In the Mondragon co-operatives, there is some change in the "social
relations of production" (that is, the power and social relationships created
through work). For example, there is much less supervision and top-down
authority in work relations. The co-operatives operated a team approach
before "team concept" was invented. However, the changes in work can be
overstated, and the actual production processes can be monotonous, with
extensive division of labour—again, perhaps reflecting the discipline of
the market. As noted above, the co-operatives know they have to further
democratize production processes and combat the alienation and apathy
some production workers experience. Nor does this model suggest that all
relations will change. It may be that women, for example, remain subju-
gated and are expected to play traditional roles, and there is nothing to say
that the system will automatically adjust to eliminate this discrimination.
These issues, though easier to raise, will have to be tackled directly.

The workers of Mondragon have taken part in solidarity strikes and, early
on in the co-operatives' life, there was an internal dispute which resulted
in sackings. But generally, unions do not have a role in Mondragon. A
social or personal committee takes over the representation of individual
grievances and other similar functions—essentially those tasks undertaken
by workplace unions in Canada. (In Canada, unions have helped members
establish company buyouts, and it does not take much imagination to see
that labour unions could play a central role in a larger restructuring of
ownership.)

Suggested Readings

Part 3 ("Contexts of Work and Economy") in *Contexts of Adult Education: Canadian Perspectives* (Fenwick et al., 2006).

Section 2, Part 1, entitled "Adult Education for Economy;" and Peruniak (Chapter 25) and Thomas (Chapter 26) in Section 3, Part 1, of *Learning for Life*.

Bakan, J. (2004). *The Corporation: The Pathological Pursuit of Profit and Power*. Toronto: Penguin Canada

Bratton, J., Helms-Mills, J., Pyrch,T. and Sawchuk, P. (2004). *Workplace Learning: A Critical Introduction*. Toronto: Garamond.

Lowe, G. (2000). *The Quality of Work: A People Centred Agenda*. Toronto: Oxford

MacLeod, G. (1998). *From Mondragon to America: Experiments in community Economic Development*. Sydney, NS: University College of Cape Breton Press.

Shields, J. (1996). Flexible work, labour market polarization, and the politics of skills training and enhancement. In Dunk, T., McBride, S., and Nelsen, R. *The Training Trap: Ideology, Training and the Labour Market*. Halifax, NS: SSS/Fernwood Publishing.

Swift, J. (1995), *Wheel of Fortune: Work and Life in the Age of Falling Expectations*.

Taylor, M. (Ed.) (1997). *Workplace Education, The Changing Landscape*.

Welton, M. (2005). *Designing the Just Learning Society: A Critical Inquiry*. Leicester: NIACE.

THE CO-OPERATIVES

Debate: Are co-operatives an alternative to traditional companies? Is the "learning" in a co-operative more developmental and democratic than in a traditional company?

Overall, Mondragon is an interesting example and, furthermore, a living example. It offers something different from capitalism, yet operates within the market economy alongside private firms. It is, therefore, a model of democratic, worker-owned firms in which workers are empowered beyond their immediate jobs and are involved (or represented through a democratic vote) in making key investment and location decisions. It is different also from schemes of wider share ownership, or profit-related pay, which are being promoted by some companies.

(A capitalist economy assumes a free capital market and a division of labour between the owners of companies and the workers; that is, between capital and labour. A market economy—essentially an economy of freely traded goods and services—can coexist with co-operatively owned companies where workers own the capital and there are no capitalists owning company shares.)

Evidence: The key evidence has been presented in the description of Mondragon co-operatives. It can be summarized by arguing that the Mondragon co-operatives operate within the limits of the marketplace, but only those who are currently producing can own and control the companies. There are no absent shareholders. (Because there are no shareholders, there would be no place for a stock exchange should this model become universal.)

What is more, the Mondragon co-operatives have a good record of job creation and retention (their original purpose), compared to traditional companies, and have spread from manufacturing production and some agriculture to banking, services, housing and retailing. They have achieved this growth because their company structure and worker involvement gave them a competitive advantage from the 1960s through the 1980s.

The range of decisions over which workers have influence is far greater than those of workers in private companies—whether or not they are "learning organizations"—and the benefits enjoyed are also more equitably distributed.

Conclusion: Mondragon is small in scale compared to some large corporations, but it does provide an interesting comparison for private companies seeking new forms of human resource management and workplace learning. It represents a more complete empowerment, a real extension of democracy (industrial democracy), workers' ownership and control, and the possibility of economic "self management." This is in contrast to the "sense" of self management and ownership claimed by Senge and others as a benefit of new participatory management techniques.

The Mondragon co-operatives are not perfect. The form of worker ownership may be more impressive than the decision-making structures at the level of production. Paul Phillips (1991) commented on Mondrgon's attempts to ensure that workers understood current policies and remained active participants in their formation through a proactive education and training program. While this might appear to be no more than other companies' "workplace learning" programs, it does offer more. Mondragon wants all members to have the tools to participate in key investment decisions and not just learn to accept key company decisions and work within those parameters. Other writers have commented on how important dialogue and debate are within Mondragon co-operatives and how this discussion rests on a bed of generally agreed values—solidarity, participation, communication and social justice (Greenwood and Santos, 1992). This emphasis on open dialogue and debate and these shared values—although sometimes claimed—are not usually actually found within private companies.

Comment: Phillips concluded his study by posing the questions of whether size can be reconciled with industrial democracy and whether or not Mondragon had found a solution through its form of representative democracy and workplace education. This question remains open as Mondragon co-operatives struggle to remain true to their worker ownership and participation principles in very difficult economic conditions. It would be a mistake to write them off; their existence and adaptations (they are constantly evolving in relation to both changes in the market and their desire to remain true to their principles) provide valuable lessons for workers everywhere. Their commitment to providing workers with a decent income, as well as worker ownership and decision making, make them an alternative to both traditionally managed and newly "re-engineered" capitalist corporations. They probably remain "the best example of democratic firms in the world today" (Ellerman, 1990, p. 212).

3
Education for Transformation

No matter what area of adult education you may work in, Michael Collins' (1991) argument that adult education should be viewed as a "thoughtful ethical commitment" is relevant and challenging. This chapter serves as an introduction to the arguments supporting "education for transformation." It will provide a context but does not attempt to provide detailed guidance to all the arguments or issues involved. Like the last chapter, it introduces a number of theories and practices in this field of study. It concludes with a case study of how an "old" social movement—labour unions—is tackling a "new" social movement issue—environmentalism. The case study prompts you to consider the implications for transformation and social change which flow from it.

This chapter is titled "Education for Transformation" because the title best fits with the mainstream American literature. It could be titled "Education for Social Change" or "Education for Community Action," or something similar. The point is that adult education (or at least a substantial part of it) has always been associated with social change, social action, social movements, community development, and participatory democracy. The title "Education for Transformation" allows us to include individual change or "perspective transformation," to use the phrase popularized by Jack Mezirow. We should also acknowledge the position adopted by Michael Welton in *Learning for Life*—that is, "social change" must include preservation and conservation of democratic values and practices that sustain life; education for transformation can be defensive.

As argued in Chapter 1, adult education emerged as a social movement, one concerned with citizenship, self-government and knowledge generation. It was an education for life, not just for livelihood. In the words of Lindeman, true adult education is social—not just social in its process, but social in its purpose. This association with progressive social ideas and action has caused problems for adult educators committed to the individualized, McCarthyite politics of the US. Therefore, some American writers have emphasized the individual as opposed to collective change and have tried to distance adult learning from social change and political action. Mezirow can be read in this context.

Michael Newman (1993), an Australian adult educator, separates Mezirow's work from a discussion of community development and social action because of its psychotherapy roots, its individualistic focus and distance from political action. While this may be a more satisfactory way of looking at Mezirow's theory—and is a perspective shared by a number of other radical adult educators (Colland and Law, 1989)—it does not fit with North American literature, which largely conflates individual and social change, down-playing the latter. Before pursuing this argument any further, we need to understand Mezirow's concepts.

Perspective Transformation

Mezirow begins by applying to adult learning the theory of knowledge that Habermas develops in *Knowledge and Human Interests*. For our purposes, Waters (1994) provides the most accessible explanation:

> Habermas conceives of knowledge as the foundation of culture (1972). The human species has at its disposal three possible means by which social organization can be established: human beings labour, they communicate, and they can exercise freedom of thought. Thus they have technical, practical and emancipatory interests. In so far as human beings are social, they can and will seek to realize one or more of these possibilities. Their interests, as a species, therefore lie in expanding this realization through the medium of work, language and power respectively. The interests in turn define three categories of possible knowledge: "information that expands our powers of technical control; interpretations that make possible the orientation of action within common traditions; and analyses that free consciousness from its dependence on hypostatized powers" (1972, p. 313). At their most scientific levels these three forms of knowledge are represented by:
>
> - the natural sciences, which operate within a methodological framework of empiricism and analysis and which enable technical control over objectified processes;
>
> - the historical-hermenueutic sciences (e.g., history, philosophy), which operate within a methodological framework of the interpretation of common experience and are orientated to a maximum intersubjectivity of mutual understanding; and
>
> - the critical social sciences (e.g., economics, sociology, political science), which may begin with an empirical-analytic framework but also can move beyond it to transform and liberate the consciousness and allow actors to free themselves from constraints that would otherwise seem natural. (Habermas 1972, pp.308–11 paraphrased in Waters, 1994, pp. 192–193).

Mezirow argues that although adult learning can be related to all three forms of knowledge, the later—the emancipatory "domain"—is particularly applicable to adult learning because self-knowledge and self-reflection can be practised by adults and can lead to transformation of consciousness.

Mezirow describes perspective transformation as "the learning process by which adults come to recognize their culturally induced dependency roles and relationships and the reasons for them and take action to overcome them" (Mezirow, 1981, p. 7). Once transformed or emancipated, adults become critically aware of the "psycho-cultural assumptions" that constrain their previous actions, opening up the possibility for new courses of action and relationships. They no longer simply fit new knowledge into existing "meaning perspectives" (a "meaning perspective" provides us with a way to look at and interpret events) determined by past experience and "psycho-cultural assumptions." ("Psycho-cultural assumptions" are socially or culturally determined and internalized, taken-for-granted views of a person's place or role in society.)

Perspective transformation also implies "a mind watching itself," in Camus' words; that is, being critically aware of one's own awareness and how it is constructed. Learners address problems through critical reflection and through examination of awareness and different meaning perspectives to see how that affects arguments and positions taken. Ideologies, power relations and cultural understandings are exposed, freeing individuals to adopt new visions and courses of action.

This is clearly a wide-ranging learning theory, better understood in relation to adult education as a whole rather than as a theory of adult education. Its emphasis on the individual learner, the psychological, on knowing oneself distances "perspective transformation" from social action. Social action may be fostered by perspective transformation or "emancipation" of the social actors, but personalized transformation does not guarantee social action. Therefore, if "adult education is social," this is not a theory of adult education, but rather a theory of adult learning.

Perspective transformation is, however, a very useful way of looking at some of the work in which adult educators engage and can lead to discussions on how to develop critical thinking (Brookfield, 1987). It can also be useful when looking at self-directed learning. It is important to stress that educational activities can bring about such changes in perspective. Mezirow (1981; 1990) and his followers emphasize internal learning processes, the "psycho-cultural," learning moments or the traumatic effect of an individual "disorienting dilemma" that often accompanies a new perspective. This emphasis can mask the role that education itself, the hard slog of knowledge exploration, plays in transforming perspectives. (This is not to deny the value of emotive or affective aspects referred to by Mezirow.)

The links between perspective transformation and Freire's "conscientization" have prompted considerable debate. ("Conscientization" refers to learning to perceive social, political, and economic forces and learning to change or resist them, as discussed in the section on Freire.) Freire is often depicted as more concerned with social change outcomes. Mezirow (1994) has characterized the difference between them as the difference between a "learning theory" (his) and an "educational philosophy" (Freire). The question adult educators are left with is: Has transformation occurred if nothing of substance changes? Those supporting Mezirow argue that his is a theory of transformation because learners do change. Those who support the view that adult education's primary purpose is to bring about change in objective conditions disagree; for them, transformation only occurs when the learners become social actors.

Before continuing our investigation of transformative adult education, we need to look more closely at Critical Social Theory, the theoretical perspective that Mezirow draws upon to formulate his learning theory.

Critical Social Theory

Critical Theory is not the same as critical thinking. While Critical Theory certainly involves critical thinking and critical reflection, which are the basic elements of critique in general, it differs from critical thinking in important ways. For our purposes the most important difference between the two is in their focus of study:

- Critical thinking explores a world of "objects" from the perspective of the individual "subject"; that is, from the viewpoint of a human being as a self-conscious, autonomous, rational agent.

- Critical Theory, on the other hand, explores a world comprised of individual "subjects" and "objects," making individual thought processes and beliefs, as well as the material "objects" human "subjects" relate to, its focus of study.

- The second difference is that, unlike critical thinking, Critical Theory maintains that social norms and conventions "distort" the understanding of individual subjects such that no amount of logical rigour or conceptual clarity (critical thinking) will remove these distortions. Hence the need for the critical social sciences and for "perspective transformation."

Critical Theory has had a major impact on educational studies. It is critical theorists such as Habermas who provided the starting point for Mezirow's theory of transformative learning. Critical Theory cannot be reduced to a neat set of propositions; it draws on a variety of philosophical and social thinkers, including Kant, Hegel, Marx, Weber, Lukacs and Freud.

The extensive writings of critical theorists such as Horkheimer, Adorno, Marcuse and Habermas are sometimes referred to as the Frankfurt School of Critical Theory (for an introduction to the Frankfurt School, see Craib, 1992; Held, 1991; Layder, 1994; Wallace and Wolfe, 1991; Waters, 1994). Questions were raised in Germany in the 1920s and 1930s about the nature and limitations of Marxist theory; in particular, its deterministic and positivist aspects which lacked practical verification (the world did not change in the way some classical Marxists predicted). These writers expressed a critical perspective on all aspects of social activity, a perspective that questioned the dominant power relations and presentations of "reality." Their concern was to explore how dominant ideologies (systems of ideas supporting social, economic and political visions) were constructed and maintained and how conflicts and contradictions were accommodated within these ideologies. In revealing the origins of these dominant (or "hegemonic") ideologies, they expected to create the conditions for raised consciousness and action to overthrow them.

Critical theorists can also be characterized as seeking to break closed systems of thought and cultural traditions which prevent analysis and re-examination. They accept that while knowledge is historically conditioned and socially perceived (what is "true" for one class of people may not be so for another), there can also be autonomous or independent "truths." They accept that their ideas are culturally and historically determined and argue that it is not possible to develop value-free knowledge. Values should be acknowledged and made clear and scholars should engage in self-criticism.

Their interdisciplinary research into the conditions for reproduction and transformation of society make their work particularly important to adult educators. An understanding of the role of culture, including popular/mass culture, the relationships between individuals and society, and how one acts on the other can help inform educators concerned with social change and defence of civil society. Considerations of such issues as the increasing integration of political and economic interests, or the formation of individual and group "identity," are important when contemplating the purposes and possibilities of adult education. Similarly, Habermas's concepts of "communicative action" (the social activity of communicating cultural understandings through which he argues society operates and develops) and the "lifeworld" (the everyday world as it is experienced by ordinary people), which emphasizes mutual understandings rather than the achievement of ends, links with the importance of "discussion" and "dialogue" in adult education.

From a post-modernist perspective, Critical Theory has been criticized as being too historical, economistic and concerned with defending the modernist pursuit of "reason." Other questions have been asked about the ability of rational discourse to change perspectives and about Critical Theory's treatment of popular culture. (For a broader discussion of post-modernism, see Craib, 1992; Easthope and McGowan, 1992; Harvey, 1989; and Layder, 1994.) Nonetheless, Critical Theory remains an important foundation (consciously or unconsciously) for adult education as can be testified by its influence in:

- Brookfield's argument for developing critical thinkers;
- Collins's plea for adult education as vocation;
- Freire's *Pedagogy of the Oppressed*;
- Hart's argument for seeing work and productivity linked to issues of gender and Third World development;
- hooks' understanding of Blacks being in and of the margin;
- Horton's view that theory flows from action towards action;

- Mezirow's theory of transformation;
- Newman's understanding of the social dynamic in *The Third Contract*;
- Smith's argument for making the everyday problematic; and
- Welton's arguments about knowledge creation in new social movements.

Education for Social Change

Since it is not possible to discuss all of the examples of adult education for social change, the next section will focus on a few examples: Freire, Horton, and British and Canadian community education.

Paulo Freire

Freire's work has been extensively referenced. The heady mixture of Catholic liberation theology, Marxism, Critical Theory and other philosophies, together with the influences from Latin America to Europe and beyond, can make his text difficult to follow. His writing style and use of metaphor reflect his cultural influences and can be obscure. Perhaps the difficulty in understanding Freire explains why his work is used as a justification for a wide variety of adult education practices. (Although Freire saw education as "education for liberation of oppressed peoples," many of the adult education practices that seek justification in his theories are far from liberating.)

Freire's work is essentially an educational philosophy, an argument about the purposes of education, and a guide to, or a way of thinking about, education. The educational methods he discusses are related to the circumstances he found himself in and should not, therefore, simply be transposed to other settings. While it is a mistake to try to reduce his work to a methodology or a series of steps, it may be helpful to look at the processes he found useful to bring about "conscientization" in his early work:

- Individuals, who may wonder at the world and accept dominant cultural myths and explanations, are brought together in a "culture circle." They are encouraged to distance themselves from the dominant culture.
- They "problematize" the world in terms of categories, or "generative themes," such as person–nature, person–person, person–culture. They then name their world, finding their own voice.
- Next, they explore these themes and describe (or re-name) the world as they and others see it. Social, economic and political structures are identified. This is a critical stage in which the

connections and interaction between individual and social
systems are recognized.

- They set out to change or transform the world, partly through
"dialogical action"; that is, action based on the language and
ideas developed by, and with, oppressed people. In so doing,
they become subjects (rather than objects) and can contribute
to the process of the humanization of the world. (This schema is
adapted from Zachariah, 1986, p. 74.)

This model of Freire's work only touches on some aspects of his ideas
and is suggested as a guide to understanding his approach to education—
education for liberation of oppressed peoples. It is not suggested as a methodology to be followed blindly. His purpose was to advance the argument
that the "culture of silence," particularly associated with illiterate peoples,
could be broken by people educating each other through the "mediation
of the world" (guided by sympathetic adult educators). By re-naming the
world, they would discover the connections between ideology and oppression and be in a situation to change it. He contrasts this type of education to
traditional knowledge transmission which he labels "banking education."

Although Freire is generally read as supporting social change, it can be
argued that Freire's conscientization process, with its emphasis on understanding one's own contribution to oppression, and his concern for liberating the oppressors is both time consuming and disarming. Such a focus
can be seen as further contributing to the oppression of those who need
to concentrate on the nature of oppression and how to change it rather
than dwell on their own complicity and the salvation of their oppressors (a
similar argument is made by Newman, 1993; 1994).

Myles Horton

Horton founded the Highlander Folk School in Tennessee in 1932. As
the name suggests, the idea of a residential adult educational facility for
working people was borrowed from the Danish Folk Schools. Horton's
(and Highlander's) educational work with labour, marginalized communities and the civil rights movement has always been dangerous. He was
committed to achieving social change through radical education and by
helping groups organize, gain confidence and identify sources of power.
This commitment brought him into direct conflict with powerful vested
interests and racists. In spite of the opposition, Highlander survived and
supported emerging social movements, making significant contributions
to social justice in the southern United States.

The Highlander educational philosophy (Horton and Freire, 1990) drew
on a variety of religious and radical sources. It is essentially experiential,
starting with the participants' own experience. Having discussed their experience, participants identify common or group experiences to try to build

a picture of social systems and then analyze how to change them. Their focus is on local conditions and the possibilities for local action. Students and teachers/facilitators share this experience and learn together. However, Horton did believe that the adult educators should accept responsibility for providing leadership to the group, which included providing their own analysis and vision. The purpose of such education is to prepare for further action—"theory flows from action toward action" (Peters and Bell, 1987, p. 258).

The participatory methods used at Highlander included music and theatre ,which are also delivered in a variety of settings. The general approach, including the outreach work described, may appear little different to that of other non-formal community education. It is, however, radical and action oriented. The measure of success was whether or not conditions changed as a result of participants' actions.

Community Education in Britain and Canada

A number of British community educational projects have been influ-ential in establishing social-change education. (In Britain, this type of education is often referred to as "social purpose" education.) Two examples include:

- the widely referenced work of Tom Lovett (1975; 1988) in working-class communities in Northern Ireland and Liverpool; and
- the work of Jane Thompson (1981; 1983) with women in Southampton.

An even more extensive range of education work for social change has emerged from the Leeds University School of Continuing Education. Leeds has been involved with:

- an extensive community education project;
- the unemployed, including a national program with "unemployment centre" workers;
- labour unions; and
- women, including immigrant women.

(Some examples of this work are discussed in Forrester and Ward, 1991; Fraser and Ward, 1988; Spencer, 1986, 1992; Taylor and Ward, 1986; and Zukas and Pillinger, 1990.) Many of the research projects of this School have a participatory base and feed directly back into educational work of the groups, unions or other social movements.

The methods used in these differing educational initiatives vary from almost entirely experiential to investigation of scholarly work and knowledge generation; from action research to skills training combined with social analysis; from day schools, residential and evening classes to outreach, partnership and distance education. The particular methods and combinations of approach depend on a number of factors, including the nature of the participants, the partnership arrangements, and the length and purposes of the programs.

Not all examples of social change education are found abroad or in the archives of Canadian practice. While the Antigonish Movement remains an important flagship of Canadian radical education traditions, there are a number of more recent examples. One such example was the Doris Marshall Institute for Education and Action in Toronto (which closed in 1995, a victim of the rise of new right ideology and funding cuts). We will conclude this thumbnail sketch of education for social change with a quote from workers at the Institute and a discussion of some of the problems they encountered. (This quote is taken from their book, *Educating for a Change* [Arnold et al., 1991], which discusses a number of methods applicable to community change education and the rationale for using the methods.) They discuss the basis of their practice:

> Traditional education is about transferring information that will reproduce values, knowledge, skills, discipline, and occupational capacities that will in turn maintain the present order of society and satisfy people's interest to "fit-in."
>
> Social change educators, on the other hand, see education as a way to help people critically evaluate and understand themselves and the world around them, to see themselves as active participants in that world. Our hopes for social transformation are ignited as people come to see themselves as creators of culture, history, and an alternative social vision.
>
> In our practice we assume that we have something to share with learners and participants about how to critically analyze the social system. At the same time we acknowledge our own positions in society and the ways that existing social arrangements limit our achievements and aspirations (Arnold, et al., 1991, p. 150).

At the same time, they acknowledge some of the difficulties:

- many people find it difficult to let go of the long-held belief that "the world of the status quo rewards them for sheer hard work and compliance";
- many of the long-held beliefs can include racism, sexism and other prejudice;
- experience itself is problematic and, sometimes, "starting from where people are at means unravelling what they hold as given";
- it can be difficult to develop a "conviction that change is possible"; and
- sometimes attempts to unearth inequality will not succeed because students have had little exposure to critical approaches that challenge the power of traditional ideas.

Any discussion of community education and education for social change should acknowledge that there are many other world-wide examples that can contribute to our understanding of this form of education. In particular, literacy and basic education programs in countries such as Tanzania and Nicaragua are examples of education for social change. There are accounts of other community-development initiatives which are grounded in indigenous peoples' experience rather than "foreign aid" (Nyerere, 1987). There are many other important theorists and scholars (such as Gramsci, 1971; Youngman, 1986; McIlroy and Westwood, 1993; or Hart, 1992), some of whom are also practitioners.

Old Social Movements (OSMs) and New Social Movements (NSMs)

Traditionally, much of the radical adult education for working people was associated with "workers' education"; that is, education for workers and primarily organized labour. Over the last 40 years, workers' education (as opposed to education for work) and labour education (education by and for labour unions) has become a minority interest within adult education, and attention has shifted to the radical potential of NSMs, such as environmental or local community groups. Organized labour, an OSM, is no longer viewed by many as a change agent; whereas NSMs are seen by some as important learning sites capable of generating new knowledge and action which could result in significant social change (Welton, 1993). We will, therefore, conclude this chapter on "education for transformation" with a review of this debate and an extended discussion of OSMs and NSMs as learning sites, focussing our attention on environmental issues.

Within adult education literature, the discussion about the importance of NSMs as learning sites focuses on their role as facilitators or providers of informal learning and education. Unions can also be considered informal learning sites, but they also provide more structured non-formal labour education for their members and activists. Welton (1993) disagrees with Finger's (1989) emphasis on NSMs as "strategies of individual survival" by arguing that they are concerned with collective goals and social purpose. However, even Welton has ignored the learning that is taking place in labour unions (OSMs) and, therefore, sees NSMs rather than OSMs as the principal defenders of the "lifeworld and ecosystem."

Introduction: The Nature of NSMs and Labour Unions

The central argument of Welton's (1993) critique of Finger (1989) is that Finger "misinterprets the values and collective struggles of the NSMs" (Welton, 1993, p. 155) and, therefore, mistakenly describes NSMs as representing "the replacement of collective goals by emerging strategies of individual survival" (Finger, 1989, p. 15). Welton describes NSMs by reference to Cohen's (1985) definition which includes "peace, feminists, ecological, and local and personal autonomy movements." Finger's analysis of NSMs is partially conditioned by his more restricted emphasis on local and personal autonomy movements as the exemplars of NSMs.

In general, this discussion supports Welton's criticism of Finger and agrees that Welton is right to chastize Finger for polarizing the old (particularly labour) and new movements so radically in order to explore new forms of individualized "life politics" learning (Welton, 1993, p. 153). He is, however, in a different way, guilty of the same offence. Welton asserts that NSMs should be interpreted "primarily as defenses of the threatened lifeworld and ecosystem" (p. 152) and, in common with other authors in the field (Larana, Johnston and Gusfield, 1994), is essentially silent on a role for organized labour. Thus collective and political representation is rescued but is left to NSMs alone. This position also accepts that NSM activists, who are essentially drawn from the middle class, can both speak for the mass of working people and act for them from their more privileged position in society.

In contrast to the position that NSMs can act for working people, it can be argued that labour unions are important workers' bulwarks, standing, in part, in defence of the "threatened lifeworld and ecosystem." It can also be argued that unions engage in a variety of educational activities and that they probably remain the single most important provider of non-vocational social-purpose adult education for working people. By examining union policy and education on the environment, it can be demonstrated that labour education is increasingly concerned with the threatened lifeworld and ecosystem.

There are perhaps three central factors that contribute to adult educator's neglect of the role of labour education:

- Unions have been critically examined and found wanting; NSMs are contrasted to the "hierarchical, centralized organization of the working-class movement" (Larana, Johnston and Gusfield, 1994, p. 9). Unions are understood to be internally bureaucratic and externally incorporated via collective bargaining into dominant society.

- Little is known about labour education in Canada, perhaps not surprising given that unions "established their own educational programs, seeking only occasional assistance from the formal educational agencies" (Thomas, 1993, p. 35). Also the union's emphasis on "tool training," essentially preparing union activists for roles within the representation and bargaining system, underscores this limited perspective on labour education.

- Many of the writers on the potency of NSMs (and by implication, the impotence of the old) are influenced by the failure of US labour to retain union membership (down to 17 percent of the non-agricultural workforce) and to influence political and social affairs.

However, these important observations about labour need to be modified; the democratic impulse, particularly at the local level, is ever present (as demonstrated by the 1993 election victories of Teamsters for a Democratic Union), as is the challenge represented by the collective values of organized labour. Unions in Canada have retained membership density and, in common with many unions in the US, are building coalitions with NSMs. The dominant union philosophy in Canada is "social unionism," as expressed by Shirley Carr, past-president of the Canadian Labour Congress (CLC). Labour unions in Canada "have always been a very effective social movement...we are prepared to pursue economic and social issues, and we always will" (Kumar and Ryan, p. 14). Another former CLC president Bob White was an advocate for the notion of linking up with other social movements—environmentalists, women's groups, aboriginal peoples, etc.—to influence the political and economic agenda (Kumar and Ryan, p. 14). Finally, labour education is much broader than the mainstream union training courses might suggest.

While these assertions can be argued further, the central remaining question to this argument is: Can an OSM, organized labour, adopt the concerns and educational practices of the NSMs, such as women's groups, peace groups or environmentalists? If we look at the educational programs offered by unions—for example, the six-level program offered by the Canadian Union of Public Employees (CUPE) discussed in Chapter 4—we can argue that much has been done in this area:

- Unions offer a number of courses addressing many NSM issues, such as employment equity and sexual or racial harassment.
- Unions have campaigned for peace and against world poverty.
- Unions have run campaigns and educational programs targeted primarily at members' behaviour outside the workplace, such as those against domestic violence and substance abuse. The Canadian Autoworkers (CAW), in particular, runs a number of short courses on these themes and has some separate programs for women, persons of colour and physically challenged members.

However, it could be argued that while unions have policies and some educational programs in these "lifeworld" and "life politics" areas, they are not that effective. In addition, in some cases, these policy positions have no force since they have not grown organically from union concerns to regulate and control the workplace and, at times, contradict those fundamental goals of unionism. For example, it is often a struggle to integrate anti-discriminatory actions with seniority rights in workplaces with established male-dominated occupations. If this is true for those issues which can be described as essentially workplace-based, then it is even more questionable as to how successful unions are in promoting issues beyond the worksite. We simply do not know if male union members who have been exposed to educational campaigns are less likely to act violently against women (although as educationalists we hope that is the case; indeed, we cannot draw any other conclusion).

Conservation versus Economic Growth

Environmentalism, which can be regarded as essentially a non-workplace issue, provides an interesting test for labour. The clash between conservation and economic growth has generally found labour siding with capital in support of development and jobs. In other cases, unions have been split in their support for conservation or development of a particular resource. There are also contrary examples where labour has provided leadership and, perhaps more importantly, muscle on some environmental issues:

- The Australian Building Workers' campaigned against uranium mining, which involved linking with transport and dock workers.
- This same group refused to pull down some older housing in Sydney to make way for "redevelopment."

However, in the popular image, loggers and pulp and sawmill workers are lined up against environmentalists and Aboriginal groups in demanding access to British Columbia's forests.

But this image is too simplistic. Unionized workers and their organizations are also concerned with longer-term employment; they do not support the despoiling tactics used by some corporations involved in resource extraction. Others live, as well as work, in the locality of a particular plant, be it mill, mine or municipal dump site. Their families, not shareholders and directors, breathe in the foul discharge from the pulp mills. There can also be a coincidence of interests, in that fewer chemicals in the plant improve the health and safety of workers and reduce the hazardous waste associated with the production process. Often this simplistic presentation of these issues is a fault of the media who do not address the diversity of opinions among union members. Just as environmentalists or Aboriginal groups can have internal differences of opinion on development issues, so, too, can organized labour. The split between pulp and paper workers (members of the Communication Energy and Paperworkers, CEP) and the woodworkers (International Woodworkers of America, IWA) over forest management in British Columbia is a prime example.

Traditionally, however, it would be accurate to charge that unions' concerns have been centred on the workplace. The priority for members is their contract—wages, benefits and conditions. Few unionists have negotiated or initiated actions around environmental questions external to the workplace. The finished product and its waste belong to the employer. Traditionally, unions have negotiated over the use and reward of their members' labour power, not its "products."

Sustainable Development

Given this context, we can now look at the following questions: How has organized labour set about developing a policy on the environment and what role has union education played? (Many of the examples and general points made in this section are taken from Shrecker, 1993.)

One of the problems for labour in dealing with environmental questions has been deciding which environmental stance to adopt. Labour has no well-developed theory to support this action. This situation changed to some extent with the publication of the Brundtland Commission's report in 1987 and the Commission's enumeration of the principles of "sustainable development." Although this is not a labour movement document, it captures many of labour's concerns with simple conservationism and melds with some existing campaigns around ensuring future work and reduction in hazardous substances. For example, the Canadian Labour Congress (CLC) has been holding conferences on jobs and the environment since 1978.

The Brundtland Commission argues that sustainable development means that current needs can be met as long as they do not affect the ability of future generations to meet their own needs. Natural resources and systems have to be maintained so that they can support advances in economic welfare into the foreseeable future. Brundtland argues that simple conservationism, that is no growth, will make the problems worse. In the extreme example, those who are poor and hungry will destroy their immediate environment in order to survive. The report also envisages that developing countries must continue to grow and argues that large benefits must be realized from that growth. Developed countries are taken to task over resource and energy use but are not expected to stagnate. Instead, the argument is made that they need to become much more resource efficient and be prepared to share their wealth.

In discussing these issues, labour has similarly argued for a blended approach to the issue of development and the environment. The following positions illustrate this point:

- The International Chemical and Energy Workers' Federation stated that "to deny the need for economic growth in a world plagued by poverty and undernourishment for the bulk of its population is as unreasonable as to insist that such growth can continue to destroy the natural habitat of mankind without interruption" (quoted in Shrecker, 1993, p. 10).

- The CAW have asserted that "workers must have the right to choose both economic security and a healthy environment for ourselves, our families and future generations" (quoted in Shrecker, 1993, p. 15).

- Ted Shrecker argued in a CLC publication, *Sustainable Development,* that this can be achieved via the sustainable development concept which "requires that growth be revived, nationally and globally, *while conserving and enhancing the resource base* on which growth depends" (Shrecker, 1993, p. 10; emphasis in the original). One of the key elements here is the recognition of the importance of renewable resources.

Adult Learning and Education

The discussion about the importance of NSMs as learning sites has focused on the understanding of their role as facilitators and providers of informal learning and education. Those who operate within these social movements learn together to identify the issues, to seek out the knowledge needed and to develop a plan to bring about change. A community-based environmental group may, for example, teach themselves about the chemicals used in particular production processes and the forms of waste associated with those chemicals and production and then, in turn, try to educate the community affected. (For a good example of a community informing themselves and developing the ability to critique experts, see Richardson, Sherman and Gismondi, 1993.)

Within NSMs, informal learning goes on all the time. The learning occurs both individually and in groups. For example, the individuals within one environmental group might learn how to organize meetings, prepare submissions, and write newsletters as an integral part of their group activities. If the group puts on a day school for themselves or the public, they are then structuring a non-formal educational event.

For the group, the processes of learning spill over into social action and range across multidisciplinary areas, which include developing people skills, processing information, and initiating and planning social action. These descriptions of NSMs as learning sites may be over-romanticized. They may underrate the importance of prior education, of expert knowledge and assistance and, indeed, overate the educational and social importance of these movements. (This assistance may take the form of formal education; to use the example from Chapter 1, a member may sign up for a course on "toxic waste disposal" offered by the local college.) However, the basic argument is that important learning is taking place and is leading to social action. A subsidiary argument, as outlined earlier, is that these NSMs have displaced the OSMs, essentially organized labour, as the provider of social-purpose adult education.

There is evidence to counter the argument that NSMs have displaced OSMs as social-purpose adult educators. Some 10,000 to 15,000 workers across Canada will engage in some form of CLC-sponsored education each year, with at least a similar number engaging in individual union-sponsored educational initiatives. The proportion of workers enrolled in union education in the US is probably one-third of those in Canada, but the absolute numbers are higher. Even in the US, labour education is the most important social-purpose education available to working people. Most of these programs straddle the training/education divide and even those courses that can clearly be labelled "tool training," such as courses that train workplace safety representatives, are designed to equip the course participants to act for other people. Union education always has a collective purpose.

In short, labour unions remain the single most important provider of non-vocational, social-purpose adult education for working people. The next question, then, is: How are labour unions educating their activists, members and the public on environmentalism?

Union Education and Environmentalism

When labour organizes around environmental questions, much of the learning that takes place is the same as learning that would have taken place in a non-labour environmental group. Labour also welds that learning to social action, which might take different forms and, in some cases, can be more effective. Labour has also learned from its previous involvement in improving the environment "inside the fence"; for example, the union may have knowledge about a particular chemical pollutant. However, that learning may, in some cases, constrain labour from reaching radical solutions on environmental questions because of the workplace emphasis on control rather than prevention. For example, workers may accept a particular chemical as long as airborne contamination is within the prescribed Threshold Limit Value, when they should really be arguing for its removal. Another characteristic of labour, which distinguishes it from NSMs, is its commitment to union educational activity.

Union education is a central part of union activity. Much of this education is "non-formal." It does not carry credentials or have links with occupational training and, even in those few instances where it does, its primary purpose remains "collective," to enhance and support union activity. This educational activity is structured, not informal, adult education. Informal adult learning also occurs in labour unions as it does in other social movements. The question still remains: What has labour done to promote environmentalism in its regular educational work? The answer to this question can be provided in part by looking at the work of the CLC.

The CLC has been committed to environmentalism and, more specifically, to sustainable development for some time. Dick Martin, former Secretary-Treasurer at the CLC, played a major role in establishing a national Environment Committee in 1987, and Dave Bennett, National Director Health and Safety, added environment to his responsibilities in 1990. Although developing education courses has not been the major focus of the CLC's campaign on the environment, to ensure its perspectives were understood by its own affiliates and their members, the CLC began developing courses for union members. A number of provincial and national conferences preceded course development. In 1993, a one-week course, Union Environmental Action, was written to be followed by materials on an introductory nine-hour course, Workers' and the Environment, and a three-hour unit, Pollution Prevention, developed primarily for inclusion in other courses. Members attending these courses also received a copy of the CLC Sustainable Development publication.

Although the publication of these materials suggests a very fixed agenda, the course program allows members to inject their own concerns and examples. However, the goal of the CLC is to get course participants to understand the key issues and struggle with the difficult problems raised. Course participants are expected to read the background information and are supplied with lists of additional readings. Many of the problems raised are open ended with a variety of policy options discussed. The CLC lists different environmental groups and notes where there have been disagreements between these groups and different unions. The possibility for establishing contacts is left open.

In addition to CLC initiatives, a number of unions have been mounting their own campaigns. Members of the pulp and paper section of CEP have a pamphlet, developed from a Swedish pulp and paper union publication, which argues for treating forests as a renewable resource and for zero discharge of chemicals. They have taken this publication to all sections of their membership and run half-day schools explaining union policy. The CAW has added a one-week course on the environment to its residential paid educational-leave program for members.

In many ways the short CLC courses, particularly the week-long Union Environmental Action course, are examples of the best traditions of workers' education in that the socio-political-economic context is provided as a basis for consideration of policy decisions and union actions. These courses can be seen as issue-based environmentalism but are not focused on a specific local concern, as might be the case with informal learning in a local environmental group. They would provide context for such learning and do not preclude local or provincial unions from mounting such an educational event. On the contrary, by sensitizing a broader constituency to the issues involved, these courses would be expected to result in more union environmental actions. Such actions might be a reaction to a particular event, such as a toxic dump site, or a new iniative taken by the union membership as a result of heightened consciousness—for example, auditing company environmental practices.

A number of features can be noted about these courses:

- the material is discussion based, beginning with students' experience to date;

- course members are provided with background material, some of which is "taught" directly during the course, with the remainder provided as background reading; and

- instructors are rarely professional educators; Canadian labour prefers to use its own members with lay and full-time officials as instructors or facilitators. To some extent, they are teaching each other and learning from labour's collective experience.

Suggested Readings

Part 1 ("Contexts in Transition") and Part 4 ("Contexts of Community and Social Movements") in *Contexts of Adult Education: Canadian Perspectives* (Fenwick et al., 2006).

See Section 2, Part 2, on "Adult Education for Transformation" in *Learning for Life*, (Scott et al., 1998). Also look at the chapters in other sections, particularly those by Collins, Grace, Miles, Scott, Stalker and Welton.

Consider some of the examples provided in *The Foundations of Adult Education in Canada, Second Edition* (Selman et al., 1998), particularly in Chapter 6.

See, especially, the chapter entitled "A Decade on the Union Rollercoaster: A Unionist's View" by D'Arcy Martin in *Learning for Life* and the sections by D'Arcy Martin on labour movement education in *The Foundations of Adult Education in Canada, Second Edition* (pp. 202–305 and pp. 393–96).

Michael Collins (1991), *Adult Education as Vocation*, is a valuable text, no matter what area of adult education you work in.

Derek Briton (1996), *The Modern Practice of Adult Education*, offers, as the subtitle suggests, a post-modern critique.

The contributions to Mike Welton's *In Defense of the Lifeworld: Critical Perspectives on Adult Education* (1995).

Chapter 3 of *Pedagogy of the Oppressed* (P. Friere, 1970) provides a fuller discussion of the conscientization process.

Anne Alexander discusses the applicability of Antigonish ideas to today in *The Antigonish Movement: Moses Coady and Adult Education Today* (1997).

OSMs and NSMs

Debate: Having reviewed labour education programs, let us return to the central question under debate: Can we still consider OSMs—in the same way as NSMs are regarded—as important learning sites and change agents, particularly in relation to environmental issues?

Evidence: The bulk of the evidence has been provided in the account in this chapter. However, it must be acknowledged that union environmental actions have not happened easily. Within one union, a group of workers can be fighting to rid their industry of a substance that is manufactured by other union members. For example, pulp workers want chlorine-free pulp; but chemical workers make the chlorine. Both groups are members of CEP. Union members, however, do not always act in their own self-interest. There have been a few actions by workers in support of cleaner technology when they have known that its adoption would threaten their jobs. An example is the Steelworkers' Local 6500 Pollution Control Committee's support for a new, cleaner smelter at Inco. Workers have never been drawn into company or government planning of new jobs; there has never been an employment fund set up to find alternative employment for those in polluting occupations. Canadian labour understands its support for sustainable development comes at a cost: "... the transition to sustainability will not always be easy or economically painless. There will be losers, and the losers are likely to be working people whose economic options are limited ..." (Shrecker, 1993, p. 119). However, given the complexity of these questions, it is important that workers develop their own voice in defence of their jobs and lifeworld. Sustainable development has to be viewed from a worker's perspective. When polluting companies are closed, workers lose jobs, and many new jobs that these workers find in the service sector are at lower rates of pay and with poorer conditions. In January, 1995, more than 20,000 workers queued up in freezing temperatures for a chance to apply for one of a few hundred jobs at General Motors. (A year later not one of the 20,000 applicants had gained a job at GM. Instead of expanding its workforce, GM boosted its profits and "downsized.") The wage for working the line was reported at $50,000—a well-paid job for workers, but a moderate income for many environmentalists. Class differences are real. Not all citizens in Canada and the United States enjoy the affluence which is assumed to apply universally by some environmentalists. As Shrecker (1994) has argued, "a lot of basic rethinking is necessary if (new) social movements that claim to be progressive are not to deserve identification as cynical defenders of privilege" (p. 15). Otherwise the pursuit of sustainable development will result in a "deepening of the gulf between rich and poor in terms both of material well being and of political power" (p. 15).

Conclusion: Canadian labour is proud of its commitment to "social unionism," but if that is to be distinguished from "business unionism," unions have to engage in promoting the breadth of concerns raised by NSM and represent the class interests of their members. Unionists may have been among the first environmentalists, but they also need to environmental concerns on a consistent basis if they are to lay claim to a green mantle. The initiatives taken so far, including those borrowed from organized labour abroad, have set them in that direction.

To favour NSMs over OSMs is a mistake which also ignores the class composition of NSMs that favour a middle-class lifeworld. The greening of unions has been positively influenced by environmental groups. However, given the diversity of such environmental groups and the need for a clearer more representative collective environmental voice—a voice which does not marginalize working class experience—perhaps it is time now that new and old social movements combine to bring about social change. Indeed, it can be argued that the building of a "radical democracy" made up from diverse NSMs has not been very successful in transforming society and that a meaningful transformation requires the social cohesion that unions, as class organizations, can bring.

Comment: The informal learning opportunities provided by union actions are not so very different from those of NSMs. Unions emphasize that individual survival is through collective actions and, as Welton (1993) has argued, NSMs are also collective actors who "cannot separate personal fulfilment from collective action" (p. 153). Although unions may be viewed as incorporated into management objectives, their relatively independent financial and external structures pull in the opposite direction. They can be free to link up with environmental groups and engage in social change activities, while learning as they go. They also have a tradition of more structured education which distinguishes them from NSMs. The courses that have been designed by the CLC and some individual unions contextualize environmental activity in a way which adult educators working with NSM rarely achieve. (Simple interpretations of Freirian methods may reject such structure as "banking knowledge," but life experience, like text itself, needs to be critically evaluated and supported by broader understandings and action.) Old and new social movements can learn together and from each other how best to protect the threatened lifeworld and ecosystem.

(A slightly longer, more theoretical version of this discussion is published in *Adult Education Quarterly* 86(1), 31–42, Fall 1995, entitled "Old social movements as learning sites: Greening labour unions and unionizing the greens.")

4
Education for Diversity

That adult education should serve the needs of diverse groups (for example, seniors, physically and mentally challenged, the unemployed), or should serve diverse causes, aims and organizations (for example, environmentalism, labour unions, leisure, cultural interests), is not always acknowledged in today's rush to make adult education and training accountable to economic objectives. Therefore, the idea that adult education should support and serve "diversity," in all these different meanings (and, thereby, serve pluralist democracy), is not always accepted.

Diversity within the adult population is a source of strength; it enriches educational experience. However, it has also been viewed as a weakness—used as a reason why particular groups have not succeeded educationally:

- "Women are no good at math and science."

- "Native students don't pay attention."

- "Black males are only good at sports."

Adult education aimed at "Canadianizing" immigrants and First Nations, like second language education, has often been construed as correcting these "deficits." Although "education for citizenship" has a proud history in Canada, it has not always been sensitive to the white, male, middle-class, Eurocentric nature of the social construction of "Canadian citizenship." Indeed, the commonly accepted concept of a "Canadian" does not reflect Canada's official multicultural policy.

Diverse Audiences, Diverse Purposes

Although adult education has been responsive to dominant political and economic aims, it has also always served diverse audiences, needs and objectives. In some cases, this "education" is constructed by the learners themselves; for example, women in the Women's Institutes or in the suffragette movement. In other cases, it is coordinated by sympathetic providers; for example, St. Francis Xavier University Extension work with co-operatives in the Antigonish Movement.

Speaking generally, adult education has made a number of important contributions to knowledge generation in a whole range of areas, such as cultural studies, women's studies, indigenous studies, labour studies, adult literacy, vocational training and community development. This creativity and diversity can be seen as being at the very foundation of adult education practice. The inter- and cross-disciplinary nature of much of this work reflects the lived experiences of adult students.

It is impossible to explore all of these topics within this book. Therefore, we will briefly review some of the issues as they apply to women in adult education, and then debate one example of diverse provision—labour education. You may want to follow up by reading Section 2, Part 3, on "Education for Diversity" in *Learning for Life* (Scott et al., 1998).

Women in Adult Education

Women form a majority of adult education students. In many cases, this reflects the previous lack of educational opportunity afforded to women. In others, it may reflect a bias towards "women's" domestic crafts in local authority provision—classes on cooking and needlecraft. In still other cases, it may reflect the fact that educational achievement is more important for the advancement of women's careers than it is for men's. But it may also represent, in part, a preference by women for social learning—a recognition that "feminist pedagogy" includes sharing, building trust relations, dialogue and story telling (some of the elements of a *Woman's Ways of Knowing*, Belenky et al., 1986). Knowledge exploration and creation, on this understanding, is a group activity— it is adult education.

Women also form a majority of the teachers within adult education. This may reflect the part-time, often insecure, status of teachers of adults. It may also reflect the "helping" or "nurturing" (socially identified as typical of women's work) associated with much of adult education work—second language teaching and adult literacy are examples. Also, similar to the argument above about women students, women teachers may be attracted to work as adult and community educators because they recognize the opportunities therein for feminist pedagogy and practice. As in many other fields where women provide the bulk of the labour force, they are not similarly represented within the administrative grades of adult education nor in the top jobs in universities. (For a broader discussion of sexism in education, see Sheehan, 1995.)

Many adult students in post-secondary institutions are subject to the "deficit model" of education typified by "adult upgrading" courses aimed at achieving a high school diploma. The idea that they could begin a distinctive adult-education program suited to their needs, which would situate their learning in their lived experiences, is not acknowledged. Instead, adult students—particularly women, working class, indigenous and immigrant adults—are treated not just as disadvantaged but as needing to "catch up." The advantage their difference gives is not recognized, and the social basis of disadvantage is individualized (see Gaskell et al., 1989, for a clear discussion of deficit and difference).

The question that arises is, Catching up to what? As Dale Spender (1980) argues, the dominant models of education are "still formulated and controlled by males" (p. 20). Dorothy Smith has explained male-dominated knowledge creation as a result of the "circle effect" whereby men talk to men, both past and present, and "a tradition is formed in this discourse of the past with the present" (1975, p. 241), a tradition which excludes women. (It can also be argued that it is a largely Eurocentric, white, middle-class, abelist and heterosexual discourse.) Even the radical models of adult education, as represented by Freire, or post-structural/ post-modern social theorists such as Foucault or Lacan, or the marriage of these into critical pedagogies by writers such as Giroux and McLaren have come under fire as male-dominated discourse (Luke and Gore, 1992). While some of this feminist critique may be overstated, its purpose is to pose a pedagogy of the possible, to celebrate "agency" or the possibility for social action, and to recognize the value of difference. The purpose of this critique—promoting agency, recognizing value in difference—is central to developing adult education as a social activity with diverse social purpose; it is particularly germane given the gender composition of adult education. Some feminist writers have themselves been criticized for promoting a white, feminist discourse that excludes minority women and does not recognize women's multiple identities (see hooks, 1981; and, for a practical application, Razacki, 1993).

Increasing Access via Prior Learning Assessment and Recognition

A discussion of prior learning assessment and recognition (PLAR) could fit into a number of different sections of this book, but given the emphasis placed on PLAR as a mechanism for increasing access to previously disadvantaged and under-represented social groups, we will analyze it here.

A movement towards granting recognition for prior learning began in the last two decades of the last century and is still gathering pace today. PLAR refers to the evaluation and acknowledgment of learning that occurs outside of formal credit-awarding training and educational programs. Increasingly, educational and training institutions are accepting PLAR as a legitimate method of gaining access to, or credit in, formal credential-bearing programs. Students are demanding that learning at work and in society be recognized within the traditional educational institutions when they seek to make the transition to formal higher education or post-secondary training. Educators are increasingly confronted by the question of how to fairly and accurately use PLAR processes to assess the educational merit of informal learning and non-formal adult education. [PLAR is the preferred term in Canada; other terms include: *prior learning assessment* (PLA), *accrediting prior learning/assessing prior learning* (APL), *accrediting prior experiential learning/assessing prior experiential learning* (APEL) and *recognition of prior learning* (RPL).] Whereas APL is sometimes reserved for transferring previous course learning and is different from APEL, PLAR will be used here to represent all these terms.)

PLAR has become a worldwide "movement" encompassing Australasia, Southern Africa, Europe and North America with an established *International Consortium for Experiential Learning*. It attracts those who see PLAR as important for increasing access for previously disadvantaged groups, but also it attracts politicians and business leaders, which suggests they may well view PLAR as a mechanism that will help turn traditional higher education towards meeting the needs, priorities and interests of the "real" world, as they see it. Adult educators have always valued student experience in the classroom, and while there is broad support for PLAR for adult students, there are concerns about processes, the transferability of knowledge, and dilution of the social, emancipatory purposes of adult education.

There are a number of ways of assessing prior learning; these include challenge exams, portfolio assessment (the most common) and demonstrations of skills and knowledge. Transfer credit is not included here since this essentially refers to the transferring of credit gained from one institution's courses to courses and programs of another. The essence of PLAR is the recognition of non-course learning gained experientially, perhaps as a consequence of volunteer or workplace activities or private self-guided study. PLAR can also include recognizing learning in non-formal adult courses and ascribing it credit. There are perhaps three basic assumptions behind PLAR:

- Significant learning can and does take place outside the classroom.
- It should be evaluated for credit by educational institutions and by the workplace for hiring and promotion.
- Education and training that force adults to repeat learning are inefficient, costly and unnecessary (HRDC, 1995, p.1).

The process of completing a portfolio is claimed as educational in itself, helping students to reflect on experience, gain confidence and redefine goals (European Commission, 2002). The process can be presented as very demanding and time consuming, but given the number of credits awarded, it is essentially time saving and is primarily concerned with reflecting on existing knowledge not new learning. Assessing portfolios is problematic and hinges on the students' writing skills and their ability to translate experience into "learning" as well as the assessor's methods and sympathies.

The process of PLAR is most often presented as theoretically unproblematic: The vast majority of research focuses on the technical questions of how to measure learning's worth and also how to persuade traditional educational institutions, and "elitist" academics, to accept PLAR credits (Thomas, 1998; European Commission, 2002). The case for PLAR fits best with technical training programs that have identifiable skills and abilities as the course objectives. Behavioural learning theories that emphasize competencies or learning outcomes best fit with this instrumental approach to training. Students are encouraged to match their skills to the course outline and outcomes and claim the credits. PLAR can be useful for workers to demonstrate that they have knowledge and skills that are needed for promotions or are applied to "laddered" skills-based job categories (for example in Australia). PLAR meets most opposition as a method of gaining credit within academic programs (particularly non-professional or applied); most courses in traditional academic programs are presented as non-instrumental since the knowledge areas, theories and learning processes of critical reading and writing on which they concentrate are outside of common discourse. Where PLAR is applicable to these programs it is often easier to grant generic course credits that match up with the broad program goals than to grant specific course credits by attempting to match up experiential learning with particular course "learning outcomes" (this broad approach is practiced in France) (European Commission, 2002).

Learning and Knowledge

PLAR raises the questions: Should all adult learning be viewed in terms of what is measurable, exchangeable and credit worthy? For example, Derek Briton has argued that the "use value" of certain knowledge is being confused with its "exchange value," what is very useful in one situation may not be "exchangeable" into course credits. It also "undervalues" experiential learning that cannot be transferred (Briton et al., 1998). This is not to claim that one kind of knowledge is superior to the other but rather that it is different. When individuals decide they need to know more about a certain topic in order to solve a particular problem at work, they are unlikely to be focused on developing critical reading and writing skills. In most cases, they are not going to seek out differing perspectives on a problem and then write an assessment of the arguments. This experiential learning can be useful when undertaking course-based learning, but it may be quite legitimate to argue that the prior learning is sufficiently different that it cannot be credited as if the applicant had undertaken the course of study (Spencer, et al. 1999). In these situations accelerated courses suited to mature adults may be most useful (many individualized distance education programs allow for student self-pacing, students can skip those sections of a course with which they are familiar and focus on those that are new—see the final chapter for a discussion of distance learning).

From a traditional adult education perspective, some of the issues involved in considering the importance of prior learning are very familiar. If we take a broad sweep of adult education, we find that credentialism has overtaken many formerly non-credential adult courses and programs. As noted in the first chapter, traditionally, adult education could be defined as outside of the "post-secondary system." Courses were offered to achieve a number of purposes, including social and community building, for example,

Canadian adult education can historically be defined as "education for citizenship" (Selman, in Scott et al., 1998; Schugurensky, in Fenwick et al., 2006). The outcome of the course was not to be measured by a "grade" but by the reflections and social actions of its participants. The learning could be individual and social, but it was not assessed for the purposes of credit. As adult educators adjusted non-credit courses to allow for awards of credit, they had to face up to many of the same issues that are associated with PLAR. A major challenge was to retain the social purposes and collective learning of traditional adult education practice while ensuring that the course would pass any external examination of its credit-worthiness. In some cases, courses were abandoned or changed significantly in order to adapt to this new learning environment. It cannot be argued that in all cases this was negative, but it can be argued that, generally speaking, the learning objectives were changed to reflect what could be tested and credentialized. This same shift in emphasis—from learning to credential —can be observed in PLAR processes.

At the core of many PLAR problems is a central contradiction of formal education that is writ even larger when considering experiential learning. The purpose of academic education is knowledge exploration and creation; the gaining of insights and understandings (in short: learning), but the outcome and importance of formal education is increasingly seen as the credential. As a result, many learners (and educators) substitute the credential for learning as their central objective. For those seeking PLAR, credit recognition can become the only goal. Instead of using PLAR to focus attention on the gaps in skills or knowledge—what is yet to be learned—the emphasis is placed on finding the fastest route to gain a credential. While this may be understandable, it may not always be in the best interests of the diverse social groups PLAR is designed to help.

PLAR emphasizes specific and generic skills as the "outcomes" of learning, rather than the gaining of insights and theoretical understandings around a particular area of knowledge or social actions. But the transference gained through PLAR into academic (as opposed to applied) credits is mainly based on what knowledge has been gained. Amongst adult education scholars, the usual starting point for a discussion about knowledge is Habermas—for example, as used by Mezirow in his theory of perspective transformation as discussed in Chapter 3. Knowledge exploration is also linked to the distinction between critical thinking skills and critical thought (as promoted in Critical Theory). Critical thought begins by questioning belief systems and by asking who benefits from dominant ideas: Its project is educational *and* emancipatory (Burbules and Berk, 1999). It is very difficult to assess these areas of knowledge through PLAR. For example, it can be argued that this approach to learning will not usually be gained at work (see previous chapter), especially given the narrow practices of our modern-day global corporations that demand loyalty and punish criticism (Klein, 2000).

As argued throughout this book, adult educators have always acknowledged the importance of adult experience in the classroom (Knowles is just one example) but knowledge gained through experience is not unproblematic. For example, Freire's work (see Chapter 3), has been used to justify PLAR. But this reading of Freire ignores his understanding that experience was a starting place, and could be very limiting and lead to a "culture of silence." His argument is for a dialogical and collective education that results in workers "renaming" the world they occupy and eventually organizing to change it. His concern with self-awareness, action and reflection is similar to feminist scholars' approaches to learning, discussed earlier, that can also be labelled experientially based but not experientially limited.

However, the academy does not have a stranglehold on what counts as knowledge—women's studies, labour studies, indigenous knowledge, cultural studies and the study of adult education all began life outside of the main halls and cloisters of the established universities. And mainstream education today still downplays or ignores the experience of minority groups in society such that their own learning about who they are and what place they occupy within the dominant culture is undertaken outside the official curriculum (Kelly, 2004). This illustrates that knowledge originating and gained outside of universities is important and in some cases is undervalued. Also, working people are capable of breaking through the workplace ideology designed to co-opt their compliance. Critical experiential learning or non-formal education (such as that provided by labour unions, see below) is relevant to some university programs.

Granting Credit

Credit can be granted on a modular or course-by-course basis or as program credits. Building PLAR into programs can have a significant impact resulting in a program tailored to meet mature-student needs. However, any claim for extensive transference of experiential learning into higher education credits needs to be critically examined if it is to gain support of academics, as Hanson has commented "rigorous though the technical requirements of PLAR may be they are of little help without a clear understanding of what they are measuring against and why" (Hanson, 1997. p. 11). Accelerating an adult student to achieve degree completion may be beneficial in lots of different ways, but it may also result in them missing out on crucial areas of knowledge, so the question of how much credit is granted and in place of what courses is important. Adult students do not have to travel the same road to a degree as a high school leaver; for example, adult life experiences may legitimately replace elective courses designed to give breadth for younger students, even if it cannot substitute for core courses. What PLAR can do is help get adult students started and advanced in their studies making higher education more accessible to previously disadvantaged groups.

Perhaps the most convincing argument for PLAR has nothing to do with whether or not a mature student has a particular knowledge that matches a higher education course. It may be possible to institute forms of PLAR that do grant advanced standing/course credits to students through the recognition that their prior learning is extensive and deserving even if it is not specifically focused on course content. The rationale for doing this is simple enough; most certificate and degree courses are designed to ground students in an area of knowledge and assume no prior knowledge beyond what could be expected from a high school student. Even when targeted at more mature students, they are mimicked on programs of study designed for graduating high school students. Adult students may not need to undergo the exact same journey to arrive at the overall understanding of a particular subject area.

For example, a student who has held a number of positions in her or his union over a number of years is likely to have insights and under-standings that go beyond those that can be expected from the average 18-year-old. Or, indeed, those from another adult student with no such experience. If she or he is enrolled in a university labour-studies program, it is likely that the student with a rich union experience can demonstrate credit-worthy knowledge relevant to the program. A similar argument can be made for students engaged in other areas of study with prior program-related areas of knowledge (social work, nursing, business, women's studies, indigenous studies, etc.). In the case of the labour studies student, it may also be possible to grant some credit for non-credit union education courses undertaken (non-formal education) as well as for the experiential knowledge gained through union activity (informal). This may result in a student doing fewer university courses, but they will still have to take some—it does not exclude the student from undertaking the hard grind of course work; from the tasks of critical reading and writing that are associated with academic work. What it does do is accept that learning outside of the academy is valuable and relevant; it may be different learning, from course-based learning but it can, nonetheless, result in valuable knowledge, some of which will be "credit worthy."

As noted above, many PLAR advocates are keen to reduce all courses to a list of "outcomes" or "competencies," because they share a limited behav-iourally influenced view of education and learning. Within the compe-tency approach, content takes second place to skills. The argument that a particular course has been put together in order to challenge a student's understanding of a particular area—or to develop critical awareness around certain issues; or to deepen insights—leaves them cold. And for some courses, it's the journey that is important, not a specific outcome. For example, a particular history or literature course may consist of reading a set of texts, carefully chosen for differing interpretations and designed to bring out contrasting opinions. Such a journey is unlikely to be travelled outside of the course. PLAR advocates should just accept that such a course is usually outside their remit. This kind of caveat is not to suggest that PLAR does not pose fundamental questions for the formal education system. For example, what exactly are the "core" areas of knowledge that constitute a particular degree; what is the relevance of "residency"; and why is a first degree usually a four-year (120 credit) program in North America? Many degree programs simply accept existing conventions while others have not undergone significant rethinking for years. Although institutions allow small variations, they essentially favour conformity, a suggestion that one "four-year" degree program should be 120 credits and another 111 and yet another 93 would create organizational apoplexy. Comparisons with other programs would become difficult to systemize. Apart from the general challenge posed by PLAR, what it also allows for is the individual candidate to challenge the course program and maybe make it fit better with the areas of skills and knowledge she or he needs, and maybe, after having earned PLAR credits, undertake a 93 credit, "four-year" degree.

While PLAR may emphasize access (dramatically illustrated in post-apartheid South Africa), there is little evidence from empirical studies conducted across Europe that it has benefited previously disadvantaged groups (European Commission, 2000). PLAR has the potential to shake up traditional teaching, but the mainstream promotion of PLAR does little to resuscitate the democratic social purposes of adult education. It has the opposite tendency; it emphasizes the argument that learning is essentially about skills and competencies useful for employment. The challenge for progressive educators today is no different to that of past adult educators. It is to marry the critical experiential learning that working people do engage in to critical theoretical knowledge within the academy—to recognize experiential knowledge when it is appropriate and build on it when needed.

An Example of Diversity: Labour Education

Does adult education have to conform to the dominant economic paradigm? Can it serve diverse, even opposite, purposes? Does all contemporary adult education have to blend with formal educational provision? The overview of labour education in Canada that follows describes one area of adult education about which little has been written. It is included here as an example of the diversity of adult education. It also illustrates the diversity of education that can exist within one category of adult education—in this case, within labour education. At the end of this review, we will revisit the questions above. (The term "union education" can be used interchangeably with "labour education" in this chapter. The term "union education" is sometime reserved for courses run directly by unions rather than by other providers.)

Introduction

> The largest public contribution to systematic adult education during the early seventies has been the financial support of the Federal Government for *labour education*...The expenditures of these organizations (labour unions) on education has also increased, making it possible for thousands of Canadian workers to acquire skills of management, decision making, and knowledge about society that otherwise would have been very hard to achieve.
>
> It is important to note that the money was not given to educational agencies, but to the labour organizations themselves. Most of these latter established their own educational programs, seeking only occasional assistance from the formal educational agencies" (Thomas, 1993, p. 35).

Alan Thomas's reference to labour education alerts Canadian adult educators to an important sphere of adult education little known to them. This may not be so surprising because, as he makes clear, labour unions undertake most labour education themselves without the assistance of professional adult educators. Although funding by the Federal Government has been cut, union-controlled labour education remains a major provider of non-formal adult education for working people—perhaps still more important than companies' "workplace learning" schemes.

A main purpose of labour education is to prepare and train union lay members to play an active role in the union. Another purpose is to educate activists and members about union policy, about changes in the union environment (such as new management techniques) or changes in labour law. Labour education is also used to develop union consciousness, to build common goals and to share organizing and campaign experience. Unions have a small full-time staff and, therefore, rely on what is essentially voluntary activity of their members to be effective at work. The labour education program is a major contributor to building an effective volunteer force. Labour education also helps to sustain and build a "labour culture," an alternative knowledge of events and society (see Martin, 1995).

Most labour union members learn about the union while on the job (what is often referred to as informal or incidental learning). They probably learn more and are most active during disputes, but they also learn from union publications and communications, from attending meetings, conferences and conventions, and from the union's educational programs. Although labour education only caters to a small number of members in any one year, it is social, as opposed to personal, education. It is designed to benefit a larger number of members because the course participants bring the education to other union members. Labour education has a social purpose—to promote and develop the union presence and purpose so as to advance the union collectively (see Taylor, 2001, for a comprehensive history of Canadian labour education).

The Extent of Labour Education

It is difficult to present an accurate picture of the extent of labour education in Canada for the following reasons:

- There is no consistent statistical data on labour education courses offered; and
- There is no clear definition of what constitutes labour education.

While labour centrals, such as the Canadian Labour Congress (CLC) and Canadian Federation of Labour (CFL), do collect information on the numbers of courses provided by their affiliates or by themselves and the number of union members attending, they do not have the resources to compile statistical reports. There is also no consistency in the reporting of educational provision by affiliates, provincial labour bodies or independent unions. Courses might be provided by a union local or a labour council or they may be offered collaboratively with local colleges. They may draw on funds provided provincially or nationally.

The CLC (60 percent of Canadian union members belong to unions affiliated with the CLC) accounted for the largest slice of Labour Canada funds. It reported that 1,496 students received assistance for 24 provincial schools in 1992–93 (this data is for both week-long "schools," which include several courses, and separate week-long courses or workshops) but estimated that between 10,000 to 15,000 union members attend courses in which the CLC was involved. If figures were added from the educational provision of individual unions and labour councils, these figures could easily be tripled, but there are dangers of double counting. For example, a course that is provided essentially for an individual union might be offered at a provincial federation of labour school which is partly funded by the CLC. However, the educational provision made by individual unions, union locals and labour councils is probably two or three times that made by the CLC and other union centrals.

There is also the question, What counts as labour education? Does an in-company course offered to union safety committee members, taught by union and management tutors, count as "labour education"? If so, does it still count if supervisors and management committee members are present? Does a two-hour union-induction program for new starters count as labour education?

Given these kinds of problems, it is probably of little value to attempt to pin down an accurate statistic of labour education in Canada. At best we can "guesstimate," based on the returns to Labour Canada, the records of individual unions, and assumptions as to what constitutes "labour education." Some of the statistics include the following:

- Labour Canada provided educational funds for the independent, non-affiliated unions in 1992–93 on the basis of a total of

454,000 members. The independents claimed 15,501 members participated in those funded courses, giving a participation rate of 3.4 percent.

- To take an example of one union, the United Food and Commercial Workers International Union (UFCW) calculates that 3,227 of its Canadian members participated in courses over an eleven-month period and another 668 members attended industrial conferences (giving a participation rate between 2 percent and 3.5 percent over one year on a membership of approximately 170,000).

- As another example, the Ontario Nurses' Association (ONA), with 50,000 members, educates 2,000 (4 percent) members per year.

Just as we can estimate the extent of labour education, we can also provide a list of items to be incorporated within a working definition of labour education. Mainstream labour education includes the following:

- courses lasting at least one half-day (thereby omitting short talks and inductions for new members);

- all weekend, evening and daytime classes up to and including the eight-week residential Labour College of Canada course;

- courses essentially controlled by the unions and targeted at their members, union representatives and officials;

- courses designed to enhance union effectiveness or develop union consciousness; and

- all courses for union members except specific "job" (vocational) training (but including courses on negotiating vocational training).

Using this definition and the statistical information available, we can guess that some 120,000 union members per year (3 percent of the total) underwent some form of labour education in Canada in the early 1990s.

Such a "guesstimate" would place Canadian labour education at a level of provision similar to that of the UK and Australia (although there is probably less study time per student in Canada than in the UK). However, it is much lower than the level of provision in Scandinavia (10 percent or more), where there are stronger traditions of union and workers' education and different relations between unions and the state.

An Overview of Labour Education

Most labour education courses provided by unions can be devided into:

- *tools* courses (for example, shop steward training, grievance handling, health and safety representative courses) (Gereluk, 2001).

- the next largest category is *issues* courses (for example, sexual harassment, racism or new human resource management strategies), which often seek to link workplace and societal issues.
- a third group of courses can be labelled *labour studies*, and they seek to examine the union context (for example, labour history, economics and politics).

Tools courses directly prepare members for active roles in the union, to become representatives of the union; tools courses are targeted at existing or potential union activists. They are provided directly by the unions, by labour federations or by union centrals (such as the Canadian Labour Congress [CLC], the UK Trade Union Congress [TUC], the Swedish Confederation of Trade Unions [LO]). Tools courses are also provided for unions by educational institutions (for example, by many of the labour studies centres across the US) and by educational institutions collaboratively with the central bodies or individual unions (for example, with colleges, universities and the Workers' Educational Association [WEA] collaborating with the TUC in Britain). They may also be provided by specialized institutions such as the now defunct Australian Trade Union Training Authority (TUTA) or South Africa's Development Institute for the Training, Support and Education of Labour (Ditsela).

Many unions layer their courses, with introductory, intermediate and advanced courses and programs. Some of the introductory tools courses lead on to issue courses (sometimes referred to as "awareness" courses), which are specifically targeted at raising awareness and union action around the issues discussed. In some cases there will not be a strict demarcation between tools and issues courses nor a requirement to undertake one before the other, but the differentiation between types (and therefore the aims and purposes) of labour education can be useful for analytical purposes.

The union movement also provides more extensive and demanding educational opportunities (labour studies) such as the Harvard Trade Union Program (Bernard, 1991) for lead officials, evening Certificate courses in the UK and the CLC's five-week residential Labour College of Canada (LCC). The LCC teaches four courses—labour history, economics, sociology and politics—at a first-year university level in a four-week block. Labour law is now taught as a one-week course in the regions.

Although the LCC uses some university educators and takes place in the University of Ottawa, it is a separate entity directly accountable to the CLC. This differs from the Harvard program with its more autonomous structure and from other US college programs and from the adult residential colleges in the UK, such as Ruskin and Northern College. These offer year-long programs and are open to union members. Similar labour studies programs can be found in other countries and within some mainstream university offerings (particularly in the US, Australia, New Zealand and Canada), although these are open to the general public. Perhaps the most innovative example of a labour studies program offered to union members is the negotiated, paid educational leave program developed by the Canadian Autoworkers (CAW) and now also offered by the Canadian Union of Postal Workers (CUPW).

The intention of the dedicated *labour studies* courses is to supplement trade union tools and issues courses with a broader educational program, and in some cases, to provide a research basis for union activity. Some universities are linking directly with unions to offer research collaborations (for example, Leeds in the UK; Oregon in the US) or study and research circles (for example, in Sweden). Although unions are usually represented on the "boards of studies" of the university- and college-offered *labour studies* programs, they are rarely union controlled. The variations in the nature, structures and delivery of labour education courses are manifest (Spencer, 2002; Bridgford and Stirling, 2000).

The differences between these types of courses are fluid. Some courses will have elements of each type in the one course; for example, an introductory course for shop stewards could have a history or political economy component and an issues section. Where unions put their emphasis may vary depending on many factors, such as the type of union philosophy advocated—business unionism (accommodative/adaptive) versus organizing model (oppositional/militant). The first philosophical approach may result in a greater emphasis on tools and less on *labour studies*.

Curriculum and teaching methods for these core labour education courses have been hotly contested over the years and have been linked in the assertion that labour education should adopt a *popular education* or *Freirian* approach. In its extreme form, it was argued that courses would have no specific course content; be experientially based; would respond only to the concerns of course participants attending a particular course,; and be led by facilitators rather than teachers. All other educational approaches were dismissed as forms of *banking education*. While this debate may have been beneficial in reminding labour educators of the importance of democratic participation both in the classroom and in the union and the links between the two, it also distracted attention from issues of course content. The need to address some of the key issues facing union members and to discuss information that may be outside of their immediate experience needs a planned course content as well as participatory methods. John McIlroy's chapters in *The Search for Enlightenment* (Simon, 1990) illustrates how the emphasis on participation can mask a retreat into technical training courses denuded of content and represent a move away from the traditions of workers' education committed to establishing an understanding of political economy among labour activists.

It is more common now for unions to offer a range of courses with different focuses and to incorporate participatory methods and experiential elements as appropriate: Some courses are essentially experiential and others are not. Mike Newman (1993) in the *Third Contract* has discussed the question of what adult educational philosophies and teaching methods are appropriate in different kinds of labour education courses, and has shown that a range of different educational approaches can be beneficial.

It should also be noted that unions in different countries do run women-only courses and courses targeted at specific groups of members; for example, CAW advertises courses for "workers of colour." The intention in these cases is to ensure those attending are not in a minority and any issues that are specific to them are not marginalized.

Other Labour Education

While *tools, issues* and *labour studies* might describe the majority of labour education, the definitions do not encompass all labour education offerings. Unions are directly involved in a number of membership education programs, some of them with a *basic skills* or vocational purpose. In some cases, union-run *literacy* and *second language* courses are tutored by fellow unionists and act as a bridge linking immigrant or illiterate workers to union concerns and publications. Similarly, unions are responsible for a number of *worker training* programs, which allow the unions to educate workers about union concerns alongside of *vocational training*. In some countries, skilled and professional unions have a long history of union-sponsored vocational training and education courses. Unions, including non-craft unions, are becoming much more proactive in responding to company restructuring and deskilling and are arguing for reskilling, skills recognition and skills profiling, as well as challenging employers to live up to their rhetoric on "pay for knowledge."

In some countries, unions have developed a comprehensive and integrated education and training program, such as Britain's UNISON Open College, which includes labour education, basic skills, *recognition of prior learning* and vocational training opportunities for all union members. In Brazil, *Programa Integrar* offers union-sponsored labour education, vocational training and educational opportunities for the unemployed and is linked to the drive to create worker-owned co-operatives. In other situations, unions are engaging in partnered workplace-learning programs, partnered with employers or other agencies (such as NGOs). Unions are also involved in worker health and safety training (this should not be confused with union safety representative tools training), which may be joint management courses, but they often allow unions to argue for a union view (safe workplace) as opposed to a management view (safe worker) of health and safety. In some cases, union-run worker health and safety training has been used as part of union organizing drives. See *Unions and Learning in a Global Economy: International and Comparative Perspectives* (Spencer, 2002) for a rich selection of international examples of labour education programs.

We should not ignore educational provision for full-time officers within our purview of labour education. There has been a growing interest, particularly in Europe, Quebec and Canada generally, in equipping full-time officers with the educational tools needed to conduct union business in a global economy.

Unions have also had some limited involvement in television productions such as *Work Week* or *Working TV* in Canada or the labour education programs broadcast in Britain in the late 1960s and early 1970s. Union representatives participate in television and radio programs in an attempt to present union perspectives, influence public opinion and educate their members. Some unions are actively involved in encouraging schools to broaden their curriculum to include labour issues by providing packages of materials and by training and providing speakers for school visits. Also, we should not ignore union-sponsored arts and cultural events such as Canada's MayWorks or Manchester, England's labour history museum.

In summary, most labour education in Canada and elsewhere consists of *tool training* and *issue* courses targeted at union activists. In addition, unions and union centrals provide *labour studies* programs, often reserved for those activists who have been through the tool and issues courses, but sometimes targeted at members generally. A few educational institutions work with unions to provide labour education (more often labour studies) programs for labour unionists across Canada. Unions are also involved in workplace literacy, worker training programs, and in televisual broadcasting, all of which are targeted at members and do include some elements of labour education.

An Example of Union Provision: CUPE's Five-Level Program

Individual unions offer a range of courses for activists. Although the particular offerings will vary, the kinds of courses offered by CUPE are broadly typical of those of other Canadian unions. CUPE's six-level education program is graded and leads to a certificate of completion for members who have undertaken the five levels of courses—including the CLC Labour College.

Courses in levels one to four are usually offered at weekends or week-long seminars and are instructed by "peer instructors" or union staff. Broadly speaking, the levels are

1. New Members and Officers
2. Steward Training
3. Collective Bargaining

4. Specialized Courses

5. Labour College/Athabasca University Distance Education Course, and Labour College Residential Program.

Level One—New Members and Officers. Level One includes a course called Our Union which is designed to provide newer members and new local unions with knowledge about CUPE and how it functions. It also shows participants how to set up and run an effective union organization, including union committees. For example, it explains the role of union officers and how to conduct meetings. Another course offered at this level is the *Financial Officer Training,* which is a course specially designed for secretary–treasurers and trustees.

Level Two—Steward Training. This level is divided into two courses. The first is Effective Stewarding, a basic course which is primarily instructed by trained rank-and-file occasional instructors. The second course is *Advanced Steward Training* which is usually presented by union staff. This course offers more analysis of contract language and arbitration cases than the "grievance handling" component of the first course.

Level Three—Collective Bargaining. Level Three offers three courses to be taken consecutively. *The Introduction to Bargaining* course attempts to demonstrate how many of the negotiating skills used in daily life relate to the collective bargaining process. It also focuses on how to develop an overall bargaining strategy to achieve specific goals. The course includes:

- how to set and pursue bargaining goals,
- dealing with the employer,
- the importance of good communication skills,
- leadership in bargaining,
- developing effective tactics,
- building support for bargaining goals, both within the local and the community,
- the right to strike, and
- presenting a settlement to the membership.

The second collective bargaining course provides an overview of the collective bargaining system as it exists in Canada today. It outlines the roles played by the three main participants—employers, unions and governments—and analyzes the strengths and weaknesses of the system. It introduces the CUPE standard agreement and deals in detail with a number of contemporary issues.

The third course deals with formulating and substantiating collective bargaining demands and helps participants use research and statistical materials. When the course is given in a seminar setting, a mock bargaining session is a component.

Level Four—Specialized Courses. Level Four is divided into three categories:

- advanced discussions of material already covered such as advanced parliamentary procedure, arbitration, public speaking and face-to-face communications;

- courses designed to broaden the understanding of the role of trade union activity in the context of Canadian and world citizenship such as *Political Action, Understanding Economics, Labour Law*; and

- all the special issue courses such as *Health-and-Safety Training, WHMIS, Pay Equity, Employment Equity, Contracting Out, Aids in the Workplace, Union Counselling.*

Level Five—Labour College. The first two categories of Level Four serve the additional purpose of preparing members for the Level 5 Labour College of Canada residential program.

Most of these courses, in the first four levels, are available at weekend seminars sponsored by CUPE District Councils. Specific courses are arranged for union locals (or groups of them). In Ontario, the Ontario division sponsors up to three large weekend seminars with 10 to 12 courses and upwards of 350 participants. CUPE National also holds three week-long schools in Ontario. Some of these courses are available on a correspondence basis as well.

Many aspects of the CUPE five-level program are replicated by other unions at local, provincial and national levels. The mix of tool training and issue courses is common to typical union education programs in Canada; however, in some unions the level-four courses on economics or labour law are left to the CLC-sponsored provincial federation of labour schools. Course offerings also reflect the problems faced by a particular industrial sector. For example, the UFCW includes courses on repetitive strain injury as well as more common health-and-safety topics. It also has programs on layoffs and closures and an extensive union-sponsored literacy program.

Professional Unions: Nurses and Teachers

A growth area for organized labour in Canada since the 1960s has been public sector professionals, some of whom are organized within existing unions but more typically are organized independently into provincial unions such as the Ontario Nurses' Association (ONA) or the British Columbia Teachers' Federation. Most of these are not affiliated to any labour central, although there has been a move towards that, for example with university faculty.

Many of the programs run by these organizations are similar to those of other unions, but some reflect professional concerns. For example, the

ONA has a program on professional responsibility which encompasses the dual accountability of nurses as employees and as professionals. The British Columbia Teachers' Federation includes courses on a *Code of Ethics* and *Violence in Schools* within their programs.

Other courses offered reflect the particular situation facing members, such as courses on *Assertiveness Training* for nurses and on *Political Lobbying* for both groups. The British Columbia Teachers' Federation, in preparation for a shift from localized to centralized bargaining, extended the availability of their education programs to include more local representatives who might be involved in contract administration.

These unions, or professional associations, face a number of problems. While the problems are not unique to professional unionism, they are common to them. These include:

- the cost involved in gathering together representatives from scattered workplaces;
- getting time off and meeting the costs of wages lost or replacement labour (for example, a supply teacher); and
- the problem of developing a "union consciousness" among members.

The British Columbia Teachers' Federation would argue that what they are trying to do is develop a critical consciousness among their members, particularly in offering general courses on educational themes. It is clear that such programs also aim to build union identity by encouraging members to identify issues on which the union should campaign. Some unions have directly tackled the problem of developing union and class consciousness through a "membership education" program.

Membership Education: The Canadian Autoworkers (CAW) PEL Program

A number of unions are running membership education courses targeted at the broader membership and not just union activists. The most distinctive and intensive is that offered by the CAW. This program, which is now emulated by the Canadian Union of Postal Workers (CUPW), is not focused narrowly on preparing representatives for collective bargaining but on promoting an understanding of the union's social and political goals (Spencer, 1992; Saul, 1994).

The CAW and its predecessor, the Canadian section of the United Auto Workers (UAW), have been running extensive educational programs for their members and activists throughout the post-war period. Since the split from the UAW, the CAW has refurbished its Family Education Centre at Port Elgin, Ontario (on the shores of Lake Huron) and overhauled its educational programs. Central to this refurbishment is the union's Paid Educational Leave (PEL) program. The program is funded by a 2 to 3 cents per member, per hour benefit negotiated in contracts with employers. The money goes into a trust fund and is used to pay for lost wages, travel, accommodation and the educational costs of the program. The bargaining unit (usually a particular local) can send as many members as its contributions allow. The program consists of four week-long residential courses, usually separated by two to three weeks back at work. The program is previewed by applicants at a weekend residential school, to which applicants' partners are invited, and commitments are made to take the full course. A PEL course would typically consist of 130 members subdivided into six groups. The union also offers the program in French. By 1996, more than 5,000 members had completed the basic CAW/PEL program.

There have been some changes in the program, but originally each week (level) of the basic four-week course had a separate theme:

- Level 1—the present as history
- Level 2—sociology
- Level 3—political economy
- Level 4—social and political change.

Some study skills (for example, basic math and reading) and union representative skills (for example, reporting and effective speaking) were built into the course. There were also committees established at the outset, from among the course members, which mirror the kind of committees operating throughout the union—substance abuse, international affairs, women, human rights, culture and recreation. These committees organize events during the course and make recommendations to the course coordinator. The course concluded with a convention (mock-conference) focusing on the wide range of issues addressed during the course and reported on by the committees.

Local Union Discussion Leaders (LUDLs) lead the sessions. These volunteers are union activists whose release can be negotiated for a particular week (their wages are paid out of the PEL trust fund) and who have received additional leadership training. In addition to training in teaching methods, these lay tutors meet annually to discuss changes in course content and updates to materials.

There is plenty of opportunity for student experience and knowledge to be used within the groups, although the approach used is material- and subject-based rather than relying only on student experience for course content. The union's purpose is to provide a broad educational experience which challenges their members to question social, economic and political structures and to review the role of unions in society. They discuss the relationship between national and international questions as well as those between union members. It is clear from talking to members that the course is an eye-opener for many participants, particularly for those who conceived of the union as having only a limited role. The experience is also social; contacts are made and members gain an understanding of different work and community situations. Articles and books are read and videos exchanged; newspapers are gutted and discussed. It is always difficult to evaluate the impact of this kind of course. The CAW contends that a majority of participants leave with a heightened union and social consciousness and that a substantial minority are prepared to take on union positions as a result.

A four-week residential membership education program is a model for the kind of PEL that can be won through negotiations. Its future, though, is dependent on what can be achieved in negotiations. A substantial number of students come from plants in the "big three" auto companies, and those companies can be affected by layoffs and staff reductions. The union is committed to extending the PEL clauses to all its contracts in all of the new sectors merging into CAW. Approximately 75 percent of bargaining units, covering 93 percent of the union's total membership, have negotiated PEL. The biggest threat to the program comes from plant closures and the continuing restructuring of the Canadian economy.

It is important to recognize that the employer has no influence over the PEL program. It is not employer-paid time off, as experienced in some joint union/management training courses. Once the contract includes a PEL clause, the money collected goes into the CAW-PEL trust fund which pays the lost wages and expenses of members who attend the course. The member receives time off without pay from the employer. There is no government influence over the educational program the union offers its members.

This program is now being emulated by CUPW, who have negotiated a three-cents-per-member levy. They used the Port Elgin facility to run a number of PEL classes alongside CAW courses in preparation for their separate CUPW program.

Internationalism: Steelworkers' Humanity Fund Educational Program

The CAW and CUPW PEL program is not the only membership education program to include international issues. A number of unions offer courses specifically on international issues, and, given the increasing globalization of capital and the growth of free trade deals, it is important to consider how unions have responded educationally to these developments. One of the most distinctive courses is that of the Steelworkers. What follows is a description of a course called *Thinking North-South* developed by the Steelworkers Humanity Fund which is taught in Steelworkers' week-long schools. Rank-and-file activists drawn from the 280 bargaining units which have contributed to the Humanity Fund spend a week together thinking about the workings of the global economy. (The following is a short summary of Marshal, 1992.)

Over 110 rank-and-file workers throughout Canada had participated in the course by 1992. Fifteen had also travelled to visit projects in El Salvador and Peru. The course was offered seven times in a two-year period, 1991 to 1992, using participatory educational methods. Participants map out the workings of the global economy, starting with their own workplace, and eventually create a complex map linking structural adjustment in the south with free trade in the north.

The instructor team, which includes worker-instructors who have done the course and travelled to other countries, has experimented with different approaches. One course included a role play of a press conference given by delegations at an international meeting on hemispheric initiatives. The "Peruvian delegation" and "Canadian delegation" made presentations on current economic policies. The "journalists" were divided into labour and mainstream press.

The course has tackled the question of how the media frames visions of the south as a recipient of charity rather than as a potential partner in solving world problems. One video used was *Simon Ngubane: Still on Strike*, a history of the South African metalworkers. (Responses to the video included: "I had no idea there was such a sophisticated trade union movement in South Africa" or "Why does TV just show us black-on-black violence instead of news on trade unions?")

In addition to teaching internationalism, some Canadian unions sponsor international educational activities. The more extensive understanding of broader national and international context is often the focus of institutional labour studies courses.

Suggested Readings

Jeff Taylor (2001), *Union learning: Canadian Labour Education in the Twentieth Century*.

Bruce Spencer (Ed.) (2002), *Unions and Learning in a Global Economy: International and Comparative Perspectives*.

See Chapters 2, 3, 4, 17, 22, 23 and 28 in *Contexts of Adult Education: Canadian Perspectives* (2006).

See Section 2, Parts 2 and 3, on "Adult Education for Economy" and "Adult Education for Diversity" in *Learning for Life* (Scott et al., 1998).

For a further discussion of women in adult education, see Chapters 19 (Joyce Stalker) and 20 (Angela Miles) in *Learning for Life* and Chapters 4 (Shauna Butterwick) and 11 (Tammy Dewar) in *The Foundations of Adult Education in Canada*, Second Edition.

See Chapter 12 entitled "A Decade on the Union Rollercoaster: A Unionist's View" by D'Arcy Martin in *Learning for Life* and the sections by D'Arcy Martin on labour movement education in *The Foundations of Adult Education in Canada*, Second Edition (pp.202-305 and pp. 393–96).

EDUCATION FOR DIVERSITY

Debate: Having reviewed labour education in Canada, let us return to our questions for debate. Does all adult education have to be formal or vocational education and training? Can it serve diverse and even opposite purposes?

Union or labour education has been divided into three areas:

- *tool training* for union representatives,
- *issue courses* which connect workplace and society, and
- *labour studies* which look at the broader context of unionism.

While these categories overlap, they are nonetheless useful for differentiating between the main purposes of particular courses and their relationship to union organization and goals. Labour education is primarily targeted at representatives or activists in the union and they normally begin with basic tool training courses and then move on to issue courses and eventually to the more extensive labour studies courses and programs. Some unions offer membership (as opposed to representative or activist) education courses and, in some cases, such courses may more accurately be described as labour studies as they examine and explain the context of labour unionism. Labour education in Canada, therefore, can be viewed as having three main purposes:

- to maintain and sustain union organization and diverse union purposes;
- to promote change of policy and organizational goals; and
- to develop union consciousness and support social action.

This education is not directly linked to vocational demands or to formal educational qualifications. It does support union organization; it also serves diverse purposes within unions and may promote views opposite to the dominant view of global companies and capital—an opposition (and organization) that may be considered essential to the maintenance of pluralist democracy in Canada.

Unions invest a lot of time and resources in education; it is clearly important to them. Other events in a unionist's life, such as a strike or participation in actual negotiations, may provide more important and direct learning opportunities than a union course because, no matter how carefully crafted, a course is removed from the actual experience. Nevertheless, unions regard education as underpinning the union effort in the workplace and in the community; so how successful is it in achieving a diversity of opinion in Canadian society?

Evidence: In addition to the material presented above, a study sponsored by the CLC in 1990 found that:

- members expected to benefit both themselves and the union by taking union courses;
- the courses helped members to become more interested in the union; and

- members were able to make better union decisions as a result of attending union courses (Vector, 1990).

Generally, members thought courses were too short but, in other ways, were content with the course experience.

While respondents felt the major impact of labour education was on their union work, others included comments on how it changed the way they saw Canadian society (this was particularly notable in respondents from the Atlantic region) and influenced them to become involved in local politics and community actions. On the evidence of this study, the CLC's labour education programs clearly worked as a promoter of "social unionism" and the programs also worked as "education." Most students wanted more educational opportunities, preferably using the same format, but with two out of three also stating they were interested in taking labour courses at home.

In conclusion, the survey enhances the perception of union officials that education supports union activism and pluralist democracy. The CLC's National Coordinator of Program Development, Danny Mallet, has argued that the diverse educational provision of Canadian unions has been a major factor in the growth of labour unionism in Canada during a period of international decline. (For example, in the last 10 years unions in Canada have retained a density of approximately 37 percent with an increasing workforce and have, therefore, increased their membership. In contrast, unions in the US, Britain, Australia and New Zealand have suffered declines in density and actual members of between a quarter and one half in the same time period.)

Conclusion: This discussion of labour education in Canada illustrates the diversity and vibrancy of current labour education. The chapter has not dealt with theoretical issues or substantive questions of educational philosophy. It is, nonetheless, clear that the purposes and methods used in some of the education programs draw inspiration from social change or community education. Labour education is, essentially, education for social purpose; it is not undertaken to earn individualized credit or vocational advantage but supports diverse union organizational needs and diversity of opinion within Canadian society. It is possible that such education could be granted credit transfer into the formal educational system. But, if non-formal labour education is to be recognized for credit, its central purpose as social education would have to remain unchanged.

5
Education in the Twenty-First Century

This final chapter looks at the kind of adult education and learning that could dominate the early decades of the twenty-first century. The application of new technologies to education and, in particular, the creation of the virtual classroom has brought about a renewed interest in distance education as a vehicle for adult learning.

Forms of distance education have a long history in adult education, but distance education has always been problematic in relation to adult learning and social adult education. Distance education has been associated with claims for "opening" up education, making it more accessible and equitable. But does distance education overcome "barriers" to education or create new ones? Is distance education synonymous with "open" education? Does it provide greater access for adult students? These issues need to be discussed before we debate whether or not distance education and the virtual classroom can sustain adult education as "social education"—social in purpose as well as process.

The chapter also blends this discussion of distance education with many of the central issues raised in the earlier chapters. Therefore, it serves as a conclusion to our discourse on the purposes of adult education.

Economic and Technological Imperatives: From Now to Eternity?

Governments are demanding more "relevance" and "accountability" from post-secondary and adult education. Essentially this is the argument for "education for economy" that we reviewed in Chapter 2—education is to serve economic purposes. Post-secondary and adult education (often grouped together with a term such as "adult learning" or "lifelong learning") are seen as key to developing the skills needed for a knowledge-based economy. Liberal adult education, including education for leisure, recreation, community development, social purpose and critical understanding is disregarded in favour of skills training and credentialism for the new economy.

Funding cuts and increased fees drive students to accept this new paradigm. Funding cuts and job insecurity also push adult educators into accepting the limits of the new model adult education. Committed adult educators look for "spaces" to work in, gaps created by contradictions in policy, opportunities available because of the actions of voluntary agencies or independent funding sources. A course such as "new technology for women" may be intended as a training course in computer use, but it may also provide opportunities to discuss the impact of new technology on women's lives. A popular course of lectures in gardening may provide funds to sustain a community course on tenants' rights. Funds available to First Nations may be the basis of a course on building First Nations communities in an urban society. A non-credit course on "understanding economics" may, with minor adjustment, become a credit course. By such means, adult educators and adult students can try to keep the spirit of adult education—its transformatory potential and social purpose—alive within the new global economistic model.

The push to introduce new technologies into education is driven by a twin belief that this will be cost effective and will mimic the use of new technologies in business, thus preparing the students for the new work world. Some also believe that new computer-mediated communications and telecommunications, that render borders meaningless, will result in a global culture and a worldwide environment favourable to corporate interests. In this belief, distance education is seen as both a process and a means to achieve these aims. How, then, should we consider this new technology-driven distance education? Can such a technology-constructed mode of education possibly remove "barriers" and achieve a more "open," "accessible" education for adults? Can distance education be social adult education, or is it doomed to only serve economic interests?

There is ample evidence of a "snowballing interest in open and distance learning" according to Anne Nicholls (1997, p. 19)—the British Education exhibition in Hong Kong advertized less than 50 offerings in 1994 but more than 400 in 1996, the most popular being MBA programs. According to the report, the Open University (OU) Business School had no overseas students before 1991, but by 1997 overseas students make up 30 percent of its enrolment (6,000 students). Tony Stapleton of the OU is quoted as claiming distance learning as "the Holy Grail of higher education" (Nicholls, 1997, p. 19). But does such expansion of distance education only represent the educational companion to economic globalization? Is distance education capable of achieving a more diverse educational purpose?

Distance Education

Distance education has always been an evolving field of educational practice: In terms of individualized study, it has moved from mail-in correspondence courses with little tutor support to carefully crafted, instructionally designed, edited and professionally printed courses with telephone and email tutor supported courses. In grouped study it has shifted from audio "teleconferenced" courses to televisual "video-conferenced" courses and now to on-line "computer conferenced" courses. Distance education is also being re-named as flexible learning, distributive learning or computer mediated communication giving birth to on-line learning, e-learning and m-learning (mobile learning).

Distance education is essentially a delivery method, and most of the more challenging issues in distance education are also issues to be found in education generally and within adult education in particular. For example, questions of access, equity and pedagogy and the overarching questions as to what are the purposes of adult learning (for economy, transformation/social change, diversity, etc.) as posed by this book. The distance education perspective adds a twist to these issues; it flavours them without substantially changing their essence. The distinctiveness of distance education is also challenged by the increasing use of on-line learning as an add-on to traditional "face-to-face" education giving traditional classrooms a distance education component.

The Move to a Virtual Classroom

The move to the electronic classroom (the most significant aspect of on-line learning) within distance education does cause us to reconsider the impact of distance education. For example: Does on-line learning move distance education from a focus on individual study towards more traditional classroom or grouped study? Does distance education, particularly the electronic classroom, enable open, critical liberal adult education? Does it facilitate authentic dialogue—the blending of experience with other knowledge—and the pursuit of social educational aims (such as the promotion of participatory democracy and citizenship)?

Adding an on-line component to an existing individualized distance education course does not have to move that course from individualized self-paced study to grouped study. The on-line component may be little more than access to Internet resources or an instructional lesson or an on-line quiz (or some other "learning object"); it does not have to include a student to instructor and/or a student to other students component. But the possibility of on-line discussions via computer conferences does open up traditional individualized distance education courses to the opportunity of a "virtual classroom." Critics of on-line learning often refer to it as moving students away from face-to-face classrooms and dialogical education, but from a traditional distance education perspective, on-line learning creates the possibility of moving students towards a classroom and increased dialogue and away from the isolation of individualized study and dialogue limited to the course materials and occasional contact with the course tutor. This may not mean that all courses become instructor-paced courses, as some self-paced courses may have "rolling" discussions that allow students to participate when they get to those sections of the courses. But clearly the on-line aspect does favour paced courses with a cohort of students moving through the courses in the same way as traditional face-to-face courses.

Some might claim that newer technologies can completely replicate the classroom or claim that "computer-mediated communication traverses the oral/written continuum and encompasses qualities associated traditionally with both forms of communication" (Harrison and Stephen, 1996, 25 drawing on Wilkins, 1991), but in most cases, computer conferencing remains essentially a written/textual practice, not "oral." Therefore, the many qualities of oral communication, and more specifically the dynamics of the real seminar room, are not present. The "best of both worlds" thesis is not therefore sustainable. There are, however, both strengths and weaknesses in using the virtual classroom. Sometimes, it may appear to be "better" and at other times "worse" than a traditional seminar classroom, but it should be noted that the interaction achieved electronically is simply different from that achieved in a traditional classroom. (It should also be noted that some academic critics of on-line learning who lambaste it for distancing students from instructional discussion ignore the "distancing" involved in mass lectures at their own institutions, see for example Noble, 2001.)

Another trend to note at this juncture is the development of on-line components in traditional courses. In a report in *Guardian Education* (MacLeod, 2002.) Dr. Yoni Ryan of Queensland University of Technology, Australia, is quoted to illustrate how on-line learning has taken off with traditional campus-based courses, rather than distance courses, partly because of the more reliable computer access: "On campus, flexible learning has become the big driver of on-line technologies, and in Australia at least, it's to accommodate the fact that more students work in the paid workforce while studying 'full-time.' It's changed the old lecture/tutorial model, to give a greater emphasis to accessing resources." And Kathy Wiles, senior adviser for e-learning at the UK's Learning and Teaching Support Network, is reported as estimating that about 20 percent of study in traditional British University courses is now e-learning. Presumably, it can be optimistically argued that whatever benefits reside in both methods of delivery can now be enjoyed in one course (a pessimist might argue the opposite—the worst aspects of both methods come to the fore.) The promotion of on-line learning is being linked to private providers, particularly in the US; business rhetoric dominates the debate and new learning institutions can be described as "not a university in any conventional sense" but as "a set of faculties, devices, and mechanisms" and students as "potential consumers" (O'Donaghue, Singh and Dorward, 2002, 520).

Removing Barriers and Enhancing Openness?

One of the benefits claimed for post-secondary distance education is that it removes "barriers" to learning and is, therefore, "open"—as suggested in the title of the British distance learning university, the "Open University," or British Columbia's "Open Learning Agency." However, "openness" and "accessibility," as they are currently understood, are not to be equated with the traditional adult education goal of providing education for participation in democratic society. Social-purpose education, leading to an enhanced participatory democracy, has been pushed to the margins of the purposes of traditional "Western" distance education. It can be argued that, given the internal institutional constraints of delivery-centred distance education institutions and systems, distance education on its own cannot remove all barriers and become truly "open" and "accessible." Open, accessible, social-purpose adult education can only be rebuilt in collaboration with other educational and community groups. In order to explore these issues, this chapter will examine the barriers to education and how to open up access in distance education.

Barriers to Education

Cross (1981) has categorized barriers to learning into three groups: institutional, situational and dispositional. Distance education can address some of the institutional barriers such as class scheduling, entrance requirements and, perhaps, fee structures. (Although the shift to user-pay in the public sector is erecting new barriers to low-income students.) It can also help to overcome many situational barriers facing students in isolated locations and with demanding family, work and community commitments. In relation to dispositional factors associated with previous learning difficulties or socio-economic factors, distance education may have few advantages. Indeed, the dependence upon written material and "independent" study of those materials may not aid students from educationally disadvantaged backgrounds or students who are used to social, dialogical learning built on experience. Cross does not give sufficient emphasis to the socially constructed barriers of gender, class and ethnicity (all categorized as situational) that open-learning institutions need to address.

A good example of commitment by a distance-learning institution to overcoming barriers to education is provided by Athabasca University's (AU) mission statement, which begins by declaring:

> Athabasca University is dedicated to the removal of barriers that traditionally restrict access to and success in university-level studies and to increasing equality of educational opportunity for all adult Canadians regardless of their geographical location and prior academic credentials.

This statement, however, is non-specific. It does not specifically identify the "barriers that traditionally restrict access." Although AU can claim some success in removing some barriers, particularly because of its policy of open entry and distance delivery, Athabasca, in common with other open universities and colleges, has not substantially increased social equality of educational opportunity. In this regard, Athabasca's performance (illustrated later) is probably only marginally better than traditional universities'.

The educational literature emphasizes the ways in which the socially constructed barriers of gender, class and ethnicity have restricted access to educational opportunity. Other factors such as physical disability, age and geographical location can also restrict access. Educationally disadvantaged groups, which include Aboriginal peoples, women (particularly low-paid, single parent and welfare recipients), working class (particularly unskilled, low-paid and unemployed), physically challenged, immigrants (particularly non-white and non-English/French speakers in a Canadian context), northern and rural residents, older students, and prisoners continue to be under-represented in post-secondary education (Ghosh and Ray, 1987; Livingstone, 1983; McIlroy, 1993).

Also, while private corporations are able to make use of colleges and universities to undertake research or training in return for relatively small funds, other institutions, including non-profit and voluntary organizations, co-operatives, and labour unions, have been poorly served by them. Generally, they are not considered to have as "legitimate" an interest in post-secondary education as private business (Bernard, 1991) nor do they have the same financial power. While there may be a range of explanations behind this observation, it, nonetheless, illustrates limited group as well as individual "access" to the resources of the colleges and universities.

Despite the previous comments, distance education, in general, can claim some successes in terms of increasing access. For instance, some distance educators have successfully targeted courses at isolated groups, such as Aboriginal communities or prisoners, and have achieved greater access for such groups than traditional institutions. Distance education has also attracted women students, who have sometimes been referred to in the literature as coming to the institution for a "second chance." For many of these women, however, learning via distance education may more accurately be considered a "first chance" to pursue a university education. For example, approximately 65 percent of AU's students are women, the majority of whom may have had some post-secondary college education but missed out on the chance to go to, or complete, university—particularly important for women given their higher correlation between earnings and educational qualification. The proportion of AU graduates that were the first in their families to get a degree is twice that of the Canadian average. (It should be noted that women students now make up 50 percent or more of the undergraduate full-time student population of Canadian universities. However, they continue to be under-represented in some areas such as science and engineering and over-represented in others such as nursing and education. There are fewer full-time Ph.D. women students, "second" degree students—law and medicine—and faculty [University of Alberta, 1992].)

It is worth noting, however, with the possible exception of indigenous students, that women students at AU are not concentrated in the disadvantaged groups—the lower paid or welfare single parent. Distance education has also provided access for those who are geographically isolated or excluded from regular classes because of shift patterns, seasonal or other kinds of work, and family and community commitments. This successful access again needs to be qualified as many of these students, although somewhat older, come from the same socio-economic groups as mainstream students.

The above demonstrates that there has been some success in meeting the objectives of open access, particularly compared to the performance of traditional universities. In addition, some features such as open year-round enrolments, comprehensive packaged materials and telephone tutoring have been successful in removing some barriers and attracting

- women;
- older students—55 percent of AU students are between the ages of 25 and 44, only 38 percent are younger than 25 years of age;
- part-time students—AU is increasingly attracting younger students who are registered as full-time students at other institutions but who take one or two AU courses to expedite program completion. Nonetheless, the overwhelming majority of AU students are studying part-time; and
- rural and northern residents—allowing students to study at a time and place of their choice.

However, much more work is needed if barriers are to be effectively removed and distance education is to become equally "open" to all socio-economic and ethnic groups. If the mission of distance education—in common with all colleges and universities—is to contribute to a "democratic" and "civilized" society (Taylor, 1993), then democratic access is key to institutional success.

Opening Up Access

How can distance education increase access to previously disadvantaged individuals and groups? It may be argued that there is no reason why distance education should necessarily be concerned with this issue, especially if "distance education" is narrowly defined and is considered in terms of "education delivered across space." In this instance, distance education is linked to the system of delivery; it reaches those unable to study because of physical distance. However, this conceptualization of distance education usually leads to the expanded argument that distance education be used to remove barriers for others whose primary barrier may not be geographic. A major reason for establishing distance education systems was to reach groups that would otherwise not be able to access learning opportunities. Achieving greater egalitarianism in education was a primary motivation for establishing the British Open University; overcoming physical problems of distance was less important.

If the first question is "Who should have access?" a second question is "Access to what?" Most distance education in western society is designed for individualized learning to acquire academic and vocational credentials. Much less is targeted for providing social purpose education (education to prepare for and facilitate change aimed at improving the social, political and economic conditions of disadvantaged groups) or even general-ized non-credit liberal adult education—education for life not livelihood (Wiltshire, 1980). It must be acknowledged, of course, that some education may serve diverse purposes, depending upon the student's own goals. Students may use a particular course to meet their individual and/or social purposes. For example, a student may enrol in a credit English course not to satisfy degree requirements but to enhance her or his participation in political and community activity.

If, however, the primary purpose of most educational endeavour is to serve the economy and it is considered to be an investment in "human capital" such that students, companies, and society will advance economi-cally (Schultz, 1961), then it could be argued that the "educational" experience is very limited and it provides little access to liberal or critical education. Given the individualized and asocial nature of the individ-ual learning experience provided by the more traditional approaches to distance education, it may be that this approach to learning is best suited to delivering the more limited kind of educational experience discussed earlier. (It must be acknowledged that computer- and video-conferencing may render the learning experience less individualized and more social, with more interaction and group learning opportunities. However, these technologies may also be less "accessible" to some.) By extension, it could be argued that distance education should perhaps be satisfied with increas-ing access to learning opportunities that serve an economic end. But such satisfaction should not mask the limited access or limited "social" education achieved. The individualized nature of much distance education should not be allowed to dictate a narrow purpose; it is possible for distance education to serve diverse and even opposite educational goals.

There is some evidence that distance educators are becoming more inter-ested in the social dimension of distance education and a little less obsessed with the latest delivery systems as ends in themselves. This observation does not mean that distance educators have embraced a broader social purpose to develop more diverse interests in and for democratic society. It does, however, provide an opening.

How then can distance education serve the social purposes of adult education in the twenty-first century? If distance education is consciously combined with more social educational forms (for example, group and co-operative learning) and if it is linked to social movements, then the social interaction and collective learning potential of an education (including experiential and critical knowledge) leading to diverse social purposes may be possible. For example, instead of emphasizing individual learning that is designed to serve a company's goals by preparing future human-resource managers, a learner may be provided with an opportunity to learn how to work with others to establish a genuinely democratic self-managed enterprise. In this example, the distance learning institution could provide vocational technical knowledge linked to the meetings of a community enterprise group. Establishing such links is difficult because it is at odds with the "manufactured consent" (to borrow Herman and Chomsky, 2002, terminology) favouring capitalist enterprise. This dominant view supports the belief that to compete in a global economy it is necessary to attract corporate investment by making a highly skilled and educated workforce available. (The actual evidence to substantiate such a view is slight; see Swift, 1995.) To mobilize distance education in support of local economy and sustainable development is to resist the corporate drive to globalization. If distance educators are to be a force for democracy, they must contest the external "reality" (recognizing the multiplicity of realities, depending upon perspective). Equally as important, they must recognize the internal constraints of the distance education institution itself.

Overcoming Internal Constraints of Distance Education

In his industrial model of distance education, Peters (1983) has addressed the internal constraints referred to earlier. He considers that distance education is similar to a form of industrial production that depends on the division of labour, mechanization, rationalization, quality control and mass distribution. It could then be argued that an increasing dependence on technology for delivery of distance education learning experiences can entrench existing social and economic forms. Reliance on capital-intensive distance education, manufactured within an industrial model, can lead to a kind of education that is even more supportive of capital investment and increasingly less accessible to educationally disadvantaged groups. The obsession with technologically advanced delivery systems and carefully structured knowledge, which Evans and Nation (1987) refer to as "instructional industrialism," works against the more creative symbiosis of knowledge and experience that is needed for social-purpose education. Concentrating on technology can mask the way education is being used to achieve student conformity and adaptation to dominant ideology.

Typically, however, the traditional views of the role of a university or college educator have combined with internal interests in delivery systems and financial constraints to push social-purpose distance education to the margins. An exception to this trend should be noted in the way distance education is organized in some economically disadvantaged countries. There, education is often targeted at social goals and, in many cases, experienced in social groups. For example, a women's health group might gather in a remote settlement where a radio link with a health educator guides their discussion. The purpose is not just to learn about women's health issues but to do so by using information drawn from the communities in which the discussions are held. Other inspiration for the kind of distance education objectives promoted here can be found in historical examples of "distance" adult education such as Frontier College, which involved worker–educators travelling to, and working and teaching in, logging and railway camps (Fitzpatrick, 1920). Yet another example is the National Farm Radio Forum which introduced agricultural and social issues for local listening and discussion groups (both examples are discussed by Selman in *The Foundations of Adult Education in Canada, Second Edition*, 1998). It is important to note that in all the examples above, discussion and learning occurred in a group context.

Modelling Education

At this stage it might be useful to look at some definitions of distance education and assess them in terms of openness and accessibility. Keegan (1980) identified six elements present in other well-established definitions of distance education:

- separation of teacher and student
- influence of an educational organization especially in planning and preparation of learning materials
- uses of technical media
- provision of two-way communication
- possibility of occasional seminars
- participation in the most industrialized form of education

In terms of delivery, this list distinguishes distance education from more traditional forms of face-to-face education. However, the criteria of "openness" does not feature in Keegan's core definition. With the exception of his reference to Peters's industrial model, this list is not particularly helpful in pursuing questions of openness and access. It hints at flexibility in delivery and recognizes that students can be at a distance from the teacher and can, therefore, overcome spacial and time barriers. However, there is no link to a broader definition of openness or accessibility.

Garrison, in common with some other writers on distance education, has supported a view that "distance education is a species of education characterized by one structural characteristic—the noncontiguity of teacher and student" (1989, p. 8). He, therefore, argues for an understanding of distance education in the broader study of education itself. His discussion of adult and distance education (pp. 103–113) is limited, however, by his concentration on "voluntarism" and "self-directed learning" as key features of adult education, features that ignore adult education's social dimension. He refers to the early experiments in adult education, which often had a distance-education component, but does not draw out the social purpose and accessibility embedded in those experiments.

If these and similar definitions of distance education are not particularly illuminating, we need to look to other educational theories. We may look to Cross (1981), for instance, who has categorized barriers to learning. However, as noted above, she does not give sufficient emphasis to the socially constructed barriers that open-learning institutions need to address. Nonetheless, she opens the door to a discussion of social education/learning as a way of overcoming such barriers as previous educational experience and subject relevance.

Next, we turn to Dewey whose social learning emphasizes the use of small groups, dialogue, emotional support, individual and group experimentation, and praxis. These are all elements that have been identified with Freirian methods and new social movements (Freire, 1970; Friedmann, 1987; Welton, 1993). These elements can be seen in juxtaposition to traditional distance learning's emphasis on serving the needs of individual learners—an emphasis that may explain the popularity of distance education amongst policy makers and "new right" politicians. The challenge for distance education is to include social learning within the delivery system. To identify the dominant form of distance education as "instructional industrialism" does not necessarily imply that it cannot be changed.

If it is accepted that these distance and other educational paradigms provide limited models of social-purpose adult education (or "education for democracy"), we have to look elsewhere. For example, Bouchier's (1987) claims for the role of "democratic groups" within a new model of radical democratic citizenship can be extended to social-purpose education, in that such groups can help form the links:

> Between everyday experience and political interpretation, providing the support and confidence an individual needs to take the step from personal to political action. Once public action is entered, it gives the experiential basis for a broader, critical view of society as it is and might be (p.149).

This expression, which resonates with other similar propositions of social change education, including Friere's (1970) conscientization, seems very distant from the everyday experience of distance-learning institutions. It is for these reasons that it could be argued that social-purpose education, education for participatory democracy, can only be rebuilt in collaboration with other educational and community groups. The internal institutional constraints of distance education work against the complete removal of barriers and the achievement of full "accessibility." Indeed, in a case study of the British Open University, Harris (1987) argued that "every kind of openness associated with distance education seems to have its opposite side, a tendency to closure, which also has to be considered" (p. 3). A simple example of this may be provided by the increased use of computer conferencing, which results in greater student interaction, but only for those who have the equipment and skills to participate. A more complex example also draws on observations regarding computer conferencing—admittedly, observations that have yet to undergo empirical investigation. Students in a computer conference may choose to discuss the "easier" aspects of a problem at the expense of the more demanding.

Three scholars from Deakin University have adopted a critical perspective on distance education similar to that which is being argued here (Evans and Nation, 1989; Evans and King, 1991). They locate distance education within education and social science. They reject a delivery-centred approach and argue that much distance education should be understood as text production and reproduction and that critical theory and critical reflection can rescue distance education from the social relations embedded in educational technology and tradition. To achieve this, students need space to discourse with the text, create their own text, and to be more self-directed and independent learners. The Deakin-edited collections include a number of case studies that address these questions and provide examples of critical practice (some of which are more convincing than others). This kind of work is also proceeding in a number of other locations, including Athabasca University, with courses designed to allow greater student choice, more open-ended projects, experientially based assignments, and interactive materials. In arguing for critical reflection, for locating study within a broader yet critical understanding of the social, Deakin and other scholars marry critical theory and praxis to some insights gained from post-modernism and so avoid too definitive ("modernist") a purpose for education. Before adopting this stance, it might be instructive to search for the purpose of education in a writer who was not troubled by post-modernist critique.

Critical Distance Education

The Deakin critique predates the shift to on-line learning: If the dialogical nature of on-line distance education is added to the arguments above, it is clear that distance education can possess the potential for critical adult education.

The virtual classroom goes beyond the limited possibilities for dialogue with the text, and perhaps a telephone tutor, offered by traditional distance education to embrace interaction with other students, small group discussion, and open dialogue with the tutor. The computer network can also aid individual contact between students, and between students and third parties (for example by using "hot-links" to other sites embedded within the electronic course materials). Thus, the educational experience is no longer isolated and individualized; the learning can become a diverse social process. If we add the Deakin critique and understanding of distance education and assert the social purposes of adult education, then the social processes of the on-line experience can enable open, critical, liberal adult education. It can facilitate authentic dialogue—the blending of experience with other knowledge—and the pursuit of social educational aims.

Electronic communication allows for easier contact within existing community or interest groups, or it can be a means by which contact can be maintained once the group is established. It can also be argued that electronic communication has called forth new social groupings, but whether these are equivalent to new social movements or narrow interest groups has still to be determined. Our interest here is not so much with the informal learning possibilities of the Internet (the "Information Super Highway" could be viewed in any case as essentially a corporate transmission conduit) but the non-formal and formal educational opportunities provided by computer-mediated conferencing and learning (for an interesting discussion of the links between non-formal and informal on-line learning see Sawchuk, 2003).

The virtual classroom is a substantial advance on, and indeed qualitatively different from, the isolated individualized learning of traditional distance education. Furthermore, when it is combined with existing community it can support social objectives and do so across a wider terrain than is possible via traditional adult or distance education means. But there is also a danger that the virtual classroom and the Internet will be fetishized. It can be used to support narrow aims and behaviourist pedagogy and may not be critically examined by its advocates. It could be argued that these technologies were developed to help achieve economic goals of training and re-education of adults rather than social adult education. However, given the shifts in funding and emphasis in educational provision for adults away from non-formal community-based provision, it is important for adult educators to consider the potential contradictions within the newly developed forms of distance education and try to exploit distance education's virtual classrooms, hallways and coffee breaks to achieve broader purposes traditionally associated with adult education (see Spencer, 2004, for a fuller discussion).

Computer-mediated learning is affecting all education. Adults, reachable via the Internet and mobile technology, are viewed as a new market opportunity by traditional educational institutions that now see their chance to be distance trainers and adult educators. Adult educators need to critically influence this form of education; they need to ensure it is properly resourced, that it is broadly based, accessible and adventurous; that it provides citizens with the information, skills and learning required for an active participatory democracy at work and in society. This is particularly important in the field of foreign policy and international relations where citizens do not have substantial direct experience but rely on media representations: Herman and Chomsky have noted that while the Internet has been valuable to dissidents and protesters "it has limitations as a critical tool" (2002, p.xvi)—an observation that cries out for the addition of an educational dimension to on-line information.

The Purposes of Adult Education, Revisited

Please note that this section draws freely from Briton, 1996.

An illuminating model for North American educators of adults (including distance adult educators) can be rediscovered in the writings of Eduard Lindeman from the 1920s through the 1940s. He warned against modernity's impersonal, atomising and inherently oppressive forces:

> Democracy is no longer to be taken for granted. The new age, dominated by science, technology and industry, calls for a re-interpretation and a reaffirmation of our democratic way of life. We have not yet adapted ourselves to an industrial civilisation. Our lives are factionalized. Our responsibilities are varied and more easily evaded. The older patterns of society from which democratic leadership emerged automatically no longer exist. Our human relations are strained; communication between professionals and laymen becomes a more hazardous undertaking. We may continue to repeat the old Eighteenth Century ideals of equality, liberty and fraternity but the world expects us to define democracy in more realistic terms. We need not forsake the old ideals but we should now undertake the task of defining democracy in the language of practice (Lindeman, 1949, p. 179).

Lindeman saw adult education as the way of "defining democracy in the language of practice" (1932, p. 70). Adult education as an "educational movement" was born of "discontent and unadjustment...a movement is social: it starts from somewhere and moves in permeating fashion through the social mass; it originates in some form of dissatisfaction and grows as consciousness of dissatisfaction become general" (1929, pp. 31–32). Lindeman distinguished between education for adults (for example, the mainstream provision of adult distance education) and adult education—

"true adult education is social education" (1947, p. 55). Adult education, he argued, was "a social process..., not...a simple device whereby knowledge is transferred from one mind to another" (1935, p. 45). Its "primary goal is not vocational. Its aim is not to teach people how to make a living but rather how to live. It offers no ulterior reward...Life is its fundamental subject matter" (1929, p. 37). His emphasis on adult education as "an instrument for social change" (1938, p. 51) envisaged adult education preparing individuals for future change, to ensure the continuation of freedom and democracy in our modern age.

A similar discussion of the role of adult education can be found in other writings in the interwar and immediate post-war periods in other countries. Perhaps the most renowned Canadian example of adult education as social education is provided by the Antigonish Movement, which combined adult education and co-operative economic development. The purpose of which was captured by Moses Coady (1939), the best-known of the Antigonish Movement's leaders, in the title of his book, *Masters of Their Own Destiny* (1939).

While it has been argued in this book that the purposes of education for adults has always been broader than "education for democratic participation" and has included "education for reproduction" (which focuses on maintaining the culture, citizenship and order) and "education for economy" (which focuses on investing in human capital, training and human-resource development), it can also be argued that education for reproduction and economy has displaced education for democracy. It is important to recognize that adults do want the skills, knowledge, vocational tools and credentials that can improve their chances in the job market and that adult distance education has an important role to play in providing these. The current emphasis of educational provision for adults is, however, much narrower and less ambitious than that envisioned by Lindeman and other pioneers. It would seem that the real purpose of adult education as social education has been forgotten and now needs to be rediscovered.

Suggested Readings

Part 5 ("Contexts in Practice") in *Contexts of Adult Education: Canadian Perspectives* (Fenwick et al., 2006).

Concluding chapter of *The Foundations of Adult Education in Canada*, Second Edition (Selman et al., 1998).

Section 3, entitled "Challenges and Future Visions," in *Learning for Life* (Scott et al., 1998).

DISTANCE EDUCATION

Debate: Accepting both the current popularity of distance education for adults and the displacement of social adult education by credentialism (as summarized by Selman et al., 1998, pp. 410–11), could distance education inherit the Lindeman mantle? Do distance educators see themselves as adult educators? Is it possible for distance education to become a similar instigator of community and economic development via social education/ learning, or is the emphasis on individualized learning and "instructional industrialism" in distance education inevitably pulling in the opposite direction?

Evidence: Social education (including dialogue, emotional support, individual and group experimentation, and praxis achieved in part via small group activity) requires both student to student, and student to tutor interaction—which may be best achieved face-to-face. As argued in Chapter 3, it also requires that students become social actors. It is the case that some interaction can occur electronically within an existing community or maintained electronically once the group is established. Some might claim that newer technologies can completely replicate the classroom, but the evidence to date would question the authenticity of electronically mediated dialogue and group social learning.

It must be acknowledged, however, that on this issue the jury is still out. It can be argued that the type of interaction achieved electronically is not the same as that from face-to-face meetings. In my experience, short comments work best in the computer conference environment; longer expositions do not. Furthermore, the asynchronous nature of some conferences works against focused discussion when individuals pursue topics tangential to the key issues. There can also be "positives." For example, the end of class or coffee break does not bring closure to a valuable discussion (See Chapter 27 by Spencer in *Learning for Life*, Scott et al., 1998, for an expanded discussion on the virtual classroom.)

While the above discussion illustrates how distance education can aid social education, the evidence at present supports the view that distance delivery alone is less capable than face-to-face methods of providing social education.

Michael Newman's (1993) review of union training in Australia emphasized that the distinctive character of union training was the existence of the "third contract"; that is, the relationship between individual union members and the union. (The links between the students and tutor is the first contract, and those between the union and tutor is the second contract.) It could be argued that where a type of "third contract" exists (for example, where students are linked in a community or environmental group), distance education can provide social education. Trying to recreate community in the electronic classroom becomes easier if the students themselves are committed to a real community. They can then use their "individualized" studies as a basis for their community based social action.

Labour education may be considered untypical, but there are other examples of the use of distance education as "social education" in community and economic development (Koul and Jenkins, 1990) or as a component in an educational mix promoting community development (Spronk, 1994), which build on existing community links. In many instances in Canada, it is colleges or local educational consortium that are taking the lead in establishing computer facilities in remote areas and using features like audiographics to link students to each other and the instructor (as was demonstrated by the Alberta Vocational College [AVC], Lesser Slave Lake in a presentation made at Athabasca University during February of 1996).

Although this chapter has discussed the limiting nature of individualized distance education, it should be acknowledged that a central strength of distance education is that it delivers education to remote communities in which many students live and work. Students, therefore, do not need to leave their home communities where their learning can be directed toward social change (even when the emphasis may be on basic maths, as in the AVC example above).

Conclusion: If one of the purposes of distance education is to provide open, accessible adult education (open to traditionally excluded individuals and groups, providing access to educational resources for those disadvantaged, and social as opposed to individualized education) and if the purpose of education generally includes encouraging critical reflection and practical democracy (such as workers' self management), then the "barrier" of distance education itself needs to be overcome. Distance education has been characterized as individualized learning delivered via "instructional industrialism" and possibly as a "contradiction in terms" (Sewart, 1983). If it is to serve democratic social purposes, these barriers (to the extent that they are real) must be reduced. More importantly, distance adult educators must consciously engage with the external social conditions of students and link with other educational and community projects to achieve open, accessible democratic education.

Comment: The future of adult education is clearly broader than that discussed here. It involves adult education and adult learning across a wide spectrum of provision, agencies, educational institutions, practitioners, and students. However, if the new models of distance education, including computer-mediated communication via the Internet and new telecommunications such as video conferencing, are to serve the broader purposes of adult education, they must also be accessible to the broader community. They must be linked to democratic community development, locally and globally, and not just to corporate global concerns. (A longer version of this discussion is published as "Removing barriers and enhancing openness: Distance education as social adult education," in *Journal of Distance Education* 10(2) 87–104, Fall 1995.)

Appendices

This book has emphasized adult education as a social activity, social in process and purpose. There are some useful books that describe various interactive social learning methods, sometimes referred to as "popular" educational techniques, such as *Educating for a Change*—from the Doris Marshal Institute (Arnold et al., 1991). However, we also need to consider the more traditional educational needs of adult learners as independent students. If you are returning to study, you may find this appendix useful, or if you are a teacher you may wish to use it with your students.

This guide for developing your learning skills is a combination of advice culled from different sources. The first version was written by Val Smith, a tutor at Leeds University in England. It was written for union members enrolled in a two-year distance-learning program. It reviews:

- Developing Your Study Skills
- Writing Essays
- Planning and Drafting a Graduate Assignment
- Keeping a Learning Journal
- Preparing a Book Review

These notes are guidelines only. You may have a different approach that works well for you. There is always more than one way to approach studying and essay writing.

If you feel you need more help with your study skills, there are a number of good texts available—one of the best is by A. Northedge, *The Good Study Guide* (1990), published by the Open University. In many locations there are also educational counsellors who run study-skills workshops.

Developing Your Study Skills

If you live alone, it may be easier to find time to study, but you still need to make time available. If you live with others, you need their support. Discuss the problems that your study may cause and try to agree on a time and place for your study.

You will find it much easier if you can organize a place—a desk—where your your can keep books and course materials. You can save time and get started right away if you don't have to get out your materials and put them away after each session. Your local library may have places to study. This may be a good alternative when you need to do some extended reading and note making or draft an essay.

Finding a time to study is the biggest problem for most adult students. It seems that no one ever has enough time for everything that needs to be done. Get a piece of paper and write out your typical week (or month, if you are on shift work or have varied activities). Commit yourself to particular times for study. Be realistic; ask yourself how much time you can set aside for study. Ten to twelve hours a week should be adequate for most courses. If necessary, you may need to cut back on other activities for a time so that you can complete the course.

If you are at home and have less than half an hour, don't try to study. Catch up on something else—wash the dishes or play with the children! If you are alone, use short periods of time for rapid reading, filing or rewriting some notes. If you are away from home—on the bus or waiting for the dentist—carry a book so you can skim read.

If you have more than half an hour, you can undertake more serious study such as note taking from a book or working through a section of your course materials. If you are tired, you might want to concentrate on reviewing material you are already familiar with, rather than tackling something new.

If you have several hours available, use the time to write a first draft of an essay, presentation or case study response. If you are reading and taking notes, you can get stale and tired after an hour or two, even with a coffee break. If this happens, change the topic or the activity. Do some filing or sorting and then return to your original study topic.

Taking Notes

Usually all of the course materials, including your own textbook, are yours to keep so feel free to write in them as you wish. Many students find it helpful to write in the margins, underline key phrases or highlight important sections. You may also want to make separate notes in a binder. Obviously, if you borrow books from the library, you will need to make separate notes on the sections that interest you.

Try to organize your work from the outset. Make notes in such a way that you can find and understand them when you need them. The notes you make for one course can help on the next course, so develop a filing system either by hardcopy or on computer.

Check the contents of the book and skim through the sections you might need, noting the page numbers. Then, read through those sections and make notes on them.

For each item you read, write down the author's name, title of the book or article, place of publication, publisher, and date of publication (for articles or chapters in an edited collection also note the first and last page numbers). For example:

Alexander, A. (1997). *The Antigonish Movement: Moses Coady and Adult Education Today*. Toronto: Thompson Educational Publishing.

You will need this information when writing a reference list for an assignment, and you will be very glad that you were clever enough to write it down when you had the book or article in your hands. If you are quoting from the book, remember to note the page numbers from which you quote.

Write down key points and ideas in the material you are reading, using subheadings and lists if you find them helpful or necessary. For example:

From page 15 of Welton, M. (1987). *Knowledge for the People*. Toronto: Oize.

The role of the state in adult education—three considerations:

1. Low profile of adult education within educational policy formulation linked to the "structural location" and the "lack of power" of some adult students.
2. In general a capitalist state does not want to promote participatory democracy.
3. Social movements can practice "participative learning" and make gains within the state.

Do not copy out long excerpts from the material you are reading. It is far more effective to write down some key material that you may wish to quote. Be sure to use quotation marks to show that you are quoting the writer's actual words. Double check the quoted material to be certain that you have recorded it correctly. It's amazingly easy to miss a word or drop a line. For example:

On page 3, Welton claims: "Adult educational thought and practice has been largely invisible to the Canadian historian."

For longer sections, you may want to photocopy the material, as it is quicker and more accurate. You can make a copy of the material for your private study, but there are copyright restrictions on how much you can copy.

Set the information out in a form that is easy to read and easy to find when you need it again.

If you are working through a set of questions in one of the units of your course, write the question in your binder first and then write out your answer. This method is better than simply numbering your responses, because it ensures that the question is always with the answer and saves you the confusion of flipping pages back and forth.

Working through Course Materials

You may have to study pre-prepared material, particularly if you are a distance-learning student. Read the introduction and objectives for each section of the material. They indicate what you should be looking for in the readings and should guide your study strategy. For example, if you are studying Chapter 1 of this book, "Education for Adults":

Objectives

After completing this first chapter you should be able to:
1. outline the aims and purposes of adult education;
2. explain and critique the term "andragogy;"
3. discuss different philosophies of adult education; and
4. relate historical examples of Canadian adult education practice.

If a list of important terms is given, that may also alert you to the key concepts.

If there are study notes for the section you are working on, read them in conjunction with the required reading for the section. Check to see that you have an understanding of the section. For anything you are not sure about, reread the relevant material. You may find that reading the entire chapter of the text, or the assigned reading, then rereading specific parts as you answer the study questions is a good strategy to follow.

Work through each segment of your course systematically, section by section. After you have completed all sections of a unit you are working on, consider some review questions, or other activities if there are any, and write out your own responses to the reading. At this point, you may wish to try to define any key terms or concepts you have come across.

If after rereading a section you have any problems with the questions, readings or assignments, make a note of them and discuss them with your fellow students or tutor.

Tips on Writing Essays

If you experience difficulty in writing essays—as many students do—you may find the following tips helpful. Most people find writing difficult, even people who have been doing it for years and who do it for a living. If you follow the tips given here, you may find the task of writing an essay a bit easier to accomplish.

The four stages to writing an essay are

- collecting information;
- planning the essay;
- writing the rough draft; and
- rereading, sorting out and writing the final essay.

Collecting Information

Collecting information may include taking notes from your own reading, or the tutoring lessons, or from discussions with others.

Collecting the information and answering questions as you go along can be fun. There is always one more book or article to read or one more source to consult. At some stage, however, you must decide that you have enough information and begin organizing the information you have.

Planning the Essay

This stage takes time. Don't be tempted to skip it and start writing. A good plan will reveal itself in the finished essay. Planning your essay will help to structure your arguments clearly and keep your information organized.

Jot down the different ideas you have for different sections. Use headings to organize your thoughts. You may want to develop a detailed outline with main headings, subheadings and lists of points made under these. Consider the different sides of the arguments presented and assemble the evidence to support the different ideas. Spread out your information and identify which points go where. Not all of the information you have collected will fit into the essay.

Don't assume that the reader of your paper has any background on the subject of your essay—provide sufficient information to allow a reader to identify the issues in question.

You may want to run some ideas past your tutor to ensure that you do not have an essay plan that is off base.

Writing the Rough Draft

Ideally, you will sit down with all your notes organized into sections and write the rough draft in one session. If you cannot do this, try to write a number of paragraphs in one sitting. Do not worry about spelling or alterations at this stage. Just try to get a rough draft of the whole essay.

For a 1,200 to 1,500 word essay, you will need eight to ten paragraphs. This includes an introduction and a conclusion (one paragraph each) and the body (six to eight paragraphs).

The introduction should be brief—usually no more than three or four sentences. It should state concisely what your essay seeks to examine and should explain the approach you intend to take. You may be able to reword the assignment question into a statement that becomes the topic of your essay. For example: *Discuss the statement that "today's unions are the product of the legal system."* This assignment can be reworded into a number of sentences clarifying the essay topic:

> The way in which unions organize in the workplace and negotiate with employers has been profoundly influenced by the legal system. However, unions are not only legal creatures, they are also voluntary associations created by working people to promote the economic and social interests of working people—they are social movements. In this essay I will examine the argument that unions are the "product of the legal system" and argue that unions need to be understood as independent associations of working people capable of acting outside of their legally prescribed role.

The body of the essay is the main section in which you must present and develop your ideas. Your essay must be solidly based on the topic in question. General statements should be supported with specific examples and evidence. Choose only information that has direct relevance to your discussion and explain what relationship exists between the concepts you are presenting and the topic of the essay. In other words, link the individual points and paragraphs back to the essay topic. Transitions between paragraphs should be smooth, and the presentation of ideas should flow easily from one paragraph to another. Sometimes the connections are established through similarities in content, sometimes through contrasts; sometimes the development is chronological, sometimes logical. You must choose whichever approach is most appropriate for your topic.

The conclusion of your essay, like the introduction, should be brief. It should summarize your ideas and present any conclusions that have emerged from your discussion. Your concluding statements should add strength and credibility to the ideas presented in your introduction. If they do, and you have supported your argument throughout, then you will have succeeded in writing a good essay. For example:

> The evidence presented does support the contention that since the 1944 PC Order 1003 unions have largely acted within their legally prescribed role. The legal support for free collective bargaining ensured, at least until the early 1970s, that

unions had a legitimate presence within the economic and social life of Canada. However, the evidence also illustrates that labour unions, and more specifically union members, retain the ability to act without regard to their legal restrictions. The independence shown by some unionists, coupled with the broader vision of some unions, should ensure that Canada's unions are not just a legally prescribed representative of labour within the bargaining system. In the context of a global economy and the pressure to further limit union activity, the interests of Canadian workers may depend on the union movement's ability to break free of legal restrictions and restore their social movement's vision and activity.

If you find the introduction difficult to start with, try to write another section. Do anything to get started. When you have a rough draft of your essay, you may want to leave it alone for a day or two. When you return to it, you should be able to take a fresh view of what you have written. This can help you recognize errors and omissions in the content, or awkwardness in style.

Rereading, Sorting Out and Writing the Final Essay

Reread your draft, sort out any muddled ideas and rewrite any awkward sections.

Copy it out. Spread it out on the page. Use subheadings if you like. Clear, simple sentences and paragraphs will help the reader understand your meaning.

If you feel your essay is a hopeless mess at this stage, don't give up or struggle on your own. Try talking to your tutor or ask someone else to read it over—remember education should be a social activity.

Don't forget to give credit for all sources of quotations and ideas. This practice not only indicates intellectual courtesy and honesty, but also enables the reader to pursue any reference that seems particularly interesting.

For the convenience of your tutor, allow fairly large margins. This will make your essay easier to read and your tutor can then insert corrections and comments. The ideal margins are approximately 4 cm (1.5 in.) at the left and 2.5 cm (1 in.) at the top, bottom, and right-hand side. A typed or printed paper is always preferred, but if you write in long-hand, please be sure your paper is legible, double-spaced and written in ink. Before submitting your essay, take the time to proofread it carefully to catch any spelling mistakes, typing errors and the like.

Planning and Drafting a Graduate Assignment

Graduate work is designed to be more demanding than college or undergraduate study, but the basic studying and writing skills are similar. Although graduate students usually have the experience of many years of studying and writing, completing a graduate paper can still be a daunting task. Very few students, or for that matter faculty, find academic writing easy. Structuring an argument, developing a critical, reflective approach to evidence and ideas, thinking theoretically and being analytical are all hard work. Writing generally improves with practice, although you will have days when your writing does not flow or you have a topic which is particularly troublesome. The notes that follow are not comprehensive; they are designed to help you think about some of the key aspects of writing graduate assignments.

Writing a good assignment requires careful, focused research of the issues. You should be thinking in terms of answering the study question from the outset. What is the central argument—or thesis—that you are expounding? What other viewpoints will you have to refute? What evidence is available to support or challenge your arguments? In many graduate courses you can choose your own topic for your term paper. Try framing the topic as a question. You will need to develop a good grasp of the issues *and* develop a point of view about them. A survey "essay" may be appropriate at some stage of your knowledge exploration, but a survey or overview will not score as highly as an original thesis that incorporates the survey material. Therefore, you should turn your topic into a question, as in this example:

> You may be interested in the topic of "adult education within Women's Institutes." If you use that as your essay heading and are simply going to describe what goes on, you may write a competent paper, but it would have no central thesis and you could not expect to score well.
>
> If you pose a question such as, "To what extent were Women's Institutes able to develop independent adult education?" then you will still write about WIs but with more purpose, since you are now exploring an argument.

Having set your question, you need to develop your own argument. If you feel that you agree with everything said about the WIs in the Welton (1987) edited text, then there may be little point in writing on that topic. If you have something original to say, and have some evidence to back it up that will demonstrate a solid analysis and the superiority of your interpretation over others, then write. For example:

SAMPLE GRADUATE MARKING SCHEME

	A+ to A-	B+ to B-	C+ to C-
Thesis	Original. Logical interpretation and criticism to establish unique perspective. Analytically superior to other interpretations.	Clearly stated. Establishes a perspective which accounts for its selection. Clear analysis.	Clearly organized and presented. Some weaknesses.
Research	Contains key and current sources. Grasps complexity of the debates. Critically reviews all sources and perspectives.	Contains appropriate, detailed data. Includes a range of sources but treated	Contains appropriate information. Includes limited range of research. Requires more sources.
Experience	Presents pros and cons of evidence. Uses detailed sources, examples and/or stats. Juxaposes social theories.	Uses evidence to reinforce points. Pro/con arguments poor. Uses some theory.	Uses evidence sparingly. Little con argument. Opinion replaces theory.

Source: This marking scheme has been adapted from the one developed by Jerry Kachur, University of Alberta.

> In reading about the WIs, you formed the view that the BC institutes were not as independent as those in Alberta. You consider that the independence of the organization reflected a number of factors, such as the particular location and farming community, the role of provincial government, the proximity of other more independent women's organizations.
>
> You want to argue that Alberta was more independent because of the existence of these variables and you are going to show how that affected the provincial WIs and their educational output.

Having determined your argument, you need to undertake (or return to) your research. You need to critically review key and recent sources, interrogating the data. You should be able to explain the complexity of debate. For example:

> The account of the government role in the life of BC Institutes reproduced in the 1925 County Life in British Columbia (see Chapter 1) provides direct evidence contrary to the argument of the Welton (1987) text. Both viewpoints need to be evaluated and interpreted—to what extent was the WI "incorporated" by the "state?"
>
> Motions proposed to the annual Alberta WI provide evidence of membership opinion and activity. They would need to be considered against other evidence and interpretations of Alberta activity to see to what extent they can be used to support your thesis. You might want to discuss whether the motions provide evidence of "counter-hegemonic" education.

A graduate paper which has all these features will receive a good grade. Grading is always a subjective activity, but in general terms, a paper that makes an argument that uses an original and interesting thesis (and research), is critical (including self-critique), theoretical, analytical, well-structured, and has a strong introduction and conclusion, will be successful.

For more information, see the chart that illustrates some of the elements included in a graduate marking scheme. It is suggestive but should, nonetheless, give you an idea of the factors which influence grading. Graduate students should score an "A" or "B," while a student who scores a "C" may be asked to rewrite the paper.

Keeping a Learning Journal

Many courses ask you to keep a "learning journal." Below is an example of a learning journal entry:

> This has been an interesting week's discussion on social purpose adult education. Prior to this course I had not heard about the Antigonish Movement. Janet's comments about the reasons why Antigonish failed got me thinking about the conditions which exist today and whether co-operative community development is a viable option in the 1990s and, if so, what should be the role of adult education.
>
> The account of Coady's work in Jarvis (1987) shows that he was fully aware of the forces of opposition and the radical nature of what he was proposing. I will have to think some more about the debate on the significance of Antigonish: Was it deflecting more radical actions which could have brought even greater social change (as argued by John) or was it real social change in itself (as argued by Mary)? I will read some more and then put an entry into the computer conference.
>
> I was particularly interested in the adult education methods used in Antigonish. I can see links between those and Freire's (other points: both Catholics, community-based education, confronting oppressive social conditions).
>
> This week I also read Fraser and Ward (1988). It is a useful account of urban community education in the Leeds/Bradford area in the UK. It provides detailed information on the work undertaken and evaluates it. Some of the ideas and examples could be applied to my own community college if only we could escape the need for "cost-recovery" on all our community programs. I will tackle this issue when I have finished the course.
>
> Final thought: this is the fifth week, I'm exhausted. That instructor expects a lot!

As you might have guessed, this is not a real journal entry, but it includes some of the elements that go towards good journal writing: reflection, commentary on learning, reminders for action and a brief summary of reading. If you want to know more, check the library for books and articles about journal writing.

Preparing a Book Review

Many courses also ask you to undertake a book review. A good book review should:

- help the reader decide if a book is worth reading;
- provide a brief overview of the contents; and
- critically evaluate the book.

The evaluation can include an assessment of:

- the strengths and weaknesses of the main arguments;
- the organization of the arguments and text;
- the quality of the ideas and scholarship;
- whether or not the author succeeds in meeting stated objectives; and
- how the book compares with other similar works.

You can conclude your review with a recommendation stating who you think would benefit from reading the book and why. If you cannot recommend it, give your reasons.

Before tackling this kind of assignment, look at some adult education journals and see how their book reviewers write reviews. You will notice a variety of approaches and come to appreciate what a good review looks like.

References

Alberta Advanced Education and Career Development (1994). *Draft White Paper,* March.

Arnold, R., Burke, B., James, C., Martin, D. and Thomas, B. (1991). *Educating for a Change.* Toronto: Doris Marshall Institute for Education and Action.

Athabasca University (1988). *Perspectives: On Adult Education.* Athabasca: Author.

Bakan, J. (2004). The Corporation: *The Pathological Pursuit of Profit and Power.* Toronto: Penguin Canada

Beattie, A. (1997). *Working People and Lifelong Learning: A Study of the Impact of An Employee Development Scheme.* Leicester, UK: NIACE

Beckstead, D. and Gellatly, G. (2003). *The Canadian Economy in Transition: The Growth and Development of New Economy Industries.* Ottawa: Minister of Industry. 11-622-MIE no.002.

Belenky, M., et al. (1986). *Women's Ways of Knowing.* New York: Basic Books.

Bernard, E. (1991). *Labour Programmes: A Challenging Partnership.* Labour/Le Travail 27, 199–207.

Boreham, N., Samurcay, R. and Fisher, M (Eds.) (2002). *Work Process Knowledge.* London: Routledge.

Bouchier, D. (1987). *Radical Citizenship: The New American Activism.* New York: Schocken Books.

Bratton, J. (1992). *Japanisation at Work.* London: Macmillan.

Bratton, J., Helms-Mills, J., Pyrch, T. and Sawchuk, P. (2004). *Workplace Learning: A Critical Introduction.* Toronto: Garamond.

Bridgford, J. and Stirling, J. (Eds.), (2000). *Trade Union Education in Europe.* Brussels: European Trade Union College.

Briton, D. (1996). *The Modern Practice of Adult Education: A Postmodern Critique.* New York: State University of New York Press.

Briton, D., Gereluk, W. and Spencer, B (1998). Prior learning assessment and recognition: Issues for adult educators, *CASAE Conference Proceedings,* Ottawa: University of Ottawa, 24-28.

Brookfield, S. (1987). *Developing Critical Thinkers.* San Francisco: Jossey–Bass.

Brookfield, S. (2005). *The Power of Critical Theory for Adult Learning and Teaching.* Maidenhead: OU Press.

Brookfield, S.D. (1986). Review of University Adult Education in England and the USA. In *Studies in the Education of Adults* (17)1.

Brown, T. (1999). *Restructuring the Workplace: Case Studies of Informal Economic Learning.* Sydney: Centre for Popular Education, University of Technology.

Burbules, N. and Berk, R. (1999). Critical thinking and critical pedagogy: Relations, differences, and limits. In T. Popkewitz, and L Fendler (eds), *Critical Theories in Education: Changing Terrains of Knowledge and Politics,* New York: Routledge, 45-65.

Chomsky, N. (1994). *Manufacturing Consent.* Montreal: Black Rose Books.

Coady, M.M. (1939). *Masters of Their Own Destiny*. New York: Harper.

Cohen, J. (1985). Strategy or identity: New theoretical paradigms and contemporary social movements. *Social Research* 52(4) 54–78.

Cohen, M. (Ed.), (2003). *Training the Excluded for Work: Access and Equity for women, Immigrants, First Nations, Youth, and People with Low Income*. Vancouver: UBC Press.

Collard, S. and Law, M. (1989). The limits of perspective transformation: A critique of Mezirow's theory. *Adult Education Quarterly* 39, 99–107.

Collins, M. (1991). *Adult Education as Vocation: A Critical Role for the Adult Educator*. London: Routledge.

Country Life in British Columbia (1925). "British Columbia Women's Institutes," Vancouver, July, No. 7.

Craib, I. (1992). *Modern Social Theory: From Parsons to Habermas*. New York: St Martin's Press.

Crane, J.M. (1987). Moses Coady and Antigonish. In Jarvis, P. (Ed.). *Twentieth Century Thinkers in Adult Education*. New York: Croom Helm.

Cross, K.P. (1981). *Adults as Learners*. San Francisco: Jossey–Bass.

Darkenwald, G. and Merriam, S. (1982). *Adult Education: Foundations of Practice*. New York: Harper and Row.

Duffy, A., Glenday, D. and Pupo, N. (1997). *Good Jobs, Bad Jobs, No Jobs: The Transformation of Work in the 21st Century*. Toronto: Harcourt Brace.

Easthope, A. and McGowan, K. (Eds.) (1992). *A Critical and Cultural Theory Reader*. Toronto: University of Toronto Press.

Elias. J.L. and Merriam, S. (1980). *Philosophical Foundations of Adult Education*. New York: Krieger.

Ellerman, D. (1990). *The Democratic Worker–Owned Firm*. Winchester: Unwin Hyman.

English, L. (Ed.), (2005). *International Encyclopedia of Adult Education*. New York: Palgrave Macmillan.

European Commission, (2002) *Social Inclusion through APEL: A Learners Perspective*. *Comparative Report*, Glasgow: Glasgow Caledonian University.

Evans, T.D. and King, B. (1991). *Beyond the Text: Contemporary Writing on Distance Education*. Geelong: Deakin University Press.

Evans, T.D. and Nation, D.E. (1987). What future for distance education? *International Council for Distance Education Bulletin*, 14.

Evans, T.D. and Nation, D.E. (Eds.) (1989). *Critical Reflections on Distance Education*. London: Falmer Press.

Fenwick, T., Nesbit, T., and Spencer, B. (Eds.) (2006). *Contexts of Adult Education: Canadian Perspectives*. Toronto: Thompson Educational.

Field, L. (2004). Rethinking "organisational learning." In G. Foley (ed,), *Dimensions of Adult Learning: Adult Education and Training in A Global Era*. (201-218). Crows Nest, New South Wales: Allen & Unwin.

Finger, M. (1989). New social movements and their implications for adult education. *Adult Education Quarterly* 40(1) 15–21.

Finkel, A. and Conrad, M. (1993). *History of the Canadian Peoples: 1867 to the Present*, vol. 2. Mississauga, Ontario: Copp Clark Pitman.

Fitzpatrick, A. (1920). *The University in Overalls*. Toronto: Frontier College.

Foley, G. (1995). Adult education and capitalist reorganization. *Studies in the Education of Adults*, 26(1) 121–143.

Foley, G. (Ed.) (2004). *Dimensions of Adult Learning: Adult Education and Training in A Global Era*. NSW, Australia: Allen & Unwin.

Forrester, K. (1999). Work-related learning and the struggle for subjectivity, *Researching Work and Learning: A First International Conference* (pp. 188-197). Leeds: School of Continuing Education, Leeds University.

Forrester, K. and Ward, K. (Eds.) (1991). *Unemployment, Education and Training*. Sacramento: Caddo Gap Press.

Fraser, L. and Ward, K. (1988). *Education from Everyday Living*. Leicester: NIACE.

Freire, P. (1970). *Pedagogy of the Oppressed*. New York: Continuum.

Friedmann, J. (1987). *Planning in the Public Domain*. Princeton: Princeton University Press.

Friesen, G. (1993). HC Pentland and continuing education at the University of Manitoba. *Labour/Le Travail* 31, 301–14.

Garrison D.R. (1989). *Understanding Distance Education*. London: Routledge.

Gaskell, J., McLaren, A. and Novogrodsky, M. (1989). *Claiming an Education: Feminism and Canadian Schools*. Toronto: Our Schools/Our Selves.

Gereluk, W. (2001). *Labour Education in Canada Today*. Athabasca, Alberta: Athabasca University. http://www.athabascau.ca/wcs/PLAR_Report.pdf

Ghosh, R. and Ray, D. (1987). *Social Change and Education in Canada*. Toronto: Harcourt Brace.

Goodway, D. (1996). E.P. Thompson and the Making of The Making of the English Working Class. In R. Taylor, *Beyond the Walls*. Leeds: Department of Adult Continuing Education, University of Leeds, 133–143.

Gramsci, A. (1971). *Selections from Prison Notebooks*. London: Lawrence & Wishart.

Greenwood, D. and Santos, J.L.G. (1992). *Industrial Democracy as Process*. Stockholm: Swedish Centre for Working Life.

Habermas, J. (1972). *Knowledge and Human Interests*. London: Heinemann. (Original work published 1968).

Hanson, K. (1997). A university perspective on PLA. *Learning Quarterly, 1*(3), 10–13.

Harris, D. (1987). *Openness and Closure in Distance Education*. Lewes: Falmer Press.

Harrison, T & Stephen, T. (Eds.). (1996). *Computer Networking and Scholarly Communication in the Twenty-First-Century University*. New York: SUNY.

Harrison, T & Stephen, T. (Eds.). (1996). *Computer Networking and Scholarly Communication in the Twenty-first-century University*. New York: SUNY.

Hart, M. (1992). *Working and Educating for Life: Feminist and International Perspectives on Adult Education*. London: Routledge.

Hart, M. (1995). Educative or miseducative work. *Canadian Journal for the Study of Adult Education* (7)1.

Harvey, D. (1989). *The Condition of Post–Modernity*. Oxford: Blackwell.

Held, D. (1991). Frankfurt school. In T. Bottomore (Ed.), *A Dictionary of Marxist Thought* (2nd Ed.). London: Basil Blackwell, 208–213.

Hennessy, T. and Sawchuk, P. (2003). Technological change in the Canadian public sector: Worker learning responses and openings for labour-centric technological development. *3rd International Conference of Researching Work and Learning*. 111-119.

Herman, E and Chomsky, N. (2002). *Manufacturing Consent: The Political Economy of the Mass Media*. New York Pantheon.

Honderich, T. (2002). *After the Terror*. Edinburgh: Edinburgh University Press.

hooks, b. (1981). *Ain't I a Woman: Black Women and Feminism*. Boston: Southend Press.

hooks, b. (1984). *Feminist Theory: From Margins to Centre*. Boston: Southend Press.

Horton, M. and Freire, P. (1990). *We Make the Road by Walking*. Philadelphia: Temple University Press.

Human Resource Development, Canada (HRDC), (1995, May) *Prior Learning Assessment Newsletter,* 1(2). Ottawa, Ontario: HRDC.

Institute for Global Futures Research. (2000). IMF recomends greater inequality in Sweden. *Global Futures Bulletin #110*. Earlville, QLD, Australia: Author.

Jackson, N. and Jordan, S. (2000). Learning for work: Contested terrain? *Studies in the Education of Adults 32* (2), 195-211.

Keegan, D.J. (1980). On defining distance education. *Distance Educa*tion 1(1).

Kelly, J. (2004). *Borrowed Identities,* New York: Peter Lange.

Kendall, D., Lothian Murray, J. and Linden, R. (2000). *Sociology in our Times: Second Canadian Edition*. Scarborough, Ontario: Nelson.

Kincheloe, J. (1999). *How Do We Tell The Workers? The Socioeconomic Foundations of Work and Vocational Education*. Boulder, Colorado: Westview Press.

Klein, J. (1989). The human costs of manufacturing reform. *Harvard Business Review,* March-April, 60-66.

Klein, N. (2000). *No Logo: Taking Aim at the Brand Bullies*. Toronto: Random House.

Knowles, M. (1973 and 1984). *The Adult Learner: A Neglected Species*. Houston: Gulf.

Koul, B. and Jenkins, J. (1990). *Distance Education, A Spectrum of Case Studies*. London: Kogan Page.

Kumar, P. and Ryan, D. (1988). *Canadian Union Movement in the 1980s: Perspectives from Union Leaders*. Kingston: McGill-Queen's University Press.

Labour Canada. (1990, December). *Evaluation of the Labour Education Progra*m. Ottawa: Author.

Larana, L., Johnston, H. and Gusfield, J. (1994). *New Social Movements: From Ideology to Identity*. Philadelphia: Temple University Press.

Layder, D. (1994). *Understanding Social Theory*. London: Sage.

Lindeman, E. (1926, reprinted 1961). *The Meaning of Adult Education*. Montreal: Harvest House.

Lindeman, E.C. (1929). The meaning of adult education. In S. Brookfield (Ed.), *Learning Democracy: Eduard Lindeman on Adult Education and Social Change*. London: Croom Helm, 1987.

Lindeman, E.C. (1932). International aspects of adult education. In S. Brookfield (Ed.), *Learning Democracy: Eduard Lindeman on Adult Education and Social Change*. London: Croom Helm, 1987.

Lindeman, E.C. (1935). The place of discussion in the learning process. In S. Brookfield (Ed.), *Learning Democracy: Eduard Lindeman on Adult Education and Social Change*. London: Croom Helm, 1987.

Lindeman, E.C. (1938). Preparing leaders in adult education. In S. Brookfield (Ed.), *Learning Democracy: Eduard Lindeman on Adult Education and Social Change*. London: Croom Helm, 1987.

Lindeman, E.C. (1947). Methods of democratic adult education. In S. Brookfield (Ed.), *Learning Democracy: Eduard Lindeman on Adult Education and Social Change*. London: Croom Helm, 1987.

Lindeman, E.C. (1949). Democracy and the meaning of education. In S. Brookfield (Ed.), *Learning Democracy: Eduard Lindeman on Adult Education and Social Change*. London: Croom Helm, 1987.

Livingstone, D. (1983). *Class, Ideologies, and Educational -Futures*. Philadelphia: Farmer Press.

Livingstone, D. (1999). Exploring the icebergs of adult learning: Findings of the first Canadian Survey of informal learning practices. *CJSAE 13* (2), 49-72.

Lovett, T. (1975). *Adult Education, Community Development and the Working Class*. London: Ward Lock Educational.

Lovett, T. (1988). *Radical Approaches to Adult Education*. London: Routledge.

Lowe, G. (2000). *The Quality of Work: A People Centred Agenda*. Toronto: Oxford

Luke, C. and Gore, J. (1992). *Feminisms and Critical Pedagogy*. London: Routledge.

Macleans. (December 30, 2002). Crooks in the boardroom (cover story).

MacLeod, D. (2002, 17 Dec.). Back to home base. *Guardian Education*. p.9

MacLeod, G. (1998). *From Mondragon to America: Experiments in community Economic Development*. Sydney, NS: University College of Cape Breton Press.

Marshall, J. (1992, October). Steelworkers humanity fund education program. *Briarpatch*, 12–19.

Marsick, V.J. (1987). New paradigms for learning in the workplace. In V.J. Marsick (Ed.), *Learning in the Workplace*. London: Croom Helm.

Marsick, V.J. (1988). Learning in the workplace: the case for reflectivity and critical reflectivity. *Adult Education Quarterly*, 4.

Marsick, V.J. and Watkins, K. (1990). *Informal and Incidental Learning in the Workplace*. London: Routledge.

Martin, D. (1995). *Thinking Union: Activism and Education in Canada's Labour Movement*. Toronto: Between the Lines.

McIlroy, J. (1993). *Access in Higher Education*. Athabasca: Athabasca University.

McIlroy, J. and Westwood, S. (Ed.), (1993). *Border Country: Raymond Williams in Adult Education*. Leicester: NIACE.

Mezirow, J. (1981). *A critical theory of adult learning and education*. Adult Education 32(1) 3-21.

Mezirow, J. (1994). Understanding transformative theory. *Adult Education Quarterly* 44(4) 222–244.

Mezirow, J. and Associates. (1990). *Fostering Critical Reflection: A Guide to Transformative Learning*. San Fransisco: Jossey–Bass.

Moye, A.M. (1993). Mondragon: Adapting co–operative structures to meet the demands of a changing environment. *Economic and Industrial Democracy* (14) 251–276.

Newman, M. (1993). *The Third Contract: Theory and Practice in Trade Union Training*. Sydney: Stewart Victor Publishing.

Newman, M. (1994). *Defining the Enemy: Adult Education in Social Action*. N.S.W: Victor Publishing.

Newsweek (1992, Sept. 7). The Cost of Quality, 48–49.

Nicholls, A. (1997, March 16). *On the Far Side of Knowledge*. Manchester: Guardian Weekly.

Noble, D. (2001). *Digital Diploma Mills: The Automation of Higher Education*. New York: Monthly Review Press.

Nyerere, J. (1978). Development is for man by man and of man. In B.H. Hall and J. Roby Kidd (Eds.), *Adult Learning: A Design for Action*. Oxford: Pergamon.

O'Donaghue, J., Singh, G. & Dorward, L. (2002). Virtual education in universities: A technological imperative. *British Journal of Educational Technology, 32* (5), 511-523.

Palmer, B.D. (1983). *Working Class Experience*. Toronto: Butterworth.

Peters, J. and Bell, B. (1987). Horton of Highlander. In P. Jarvis (Ed.), *Twentieth Century Thinkers in Adult Education*. London: Croom Helm.

Peters, O. (1983). Distance teaching and industrial production: A comparative interpretation in outline. In D. Sewart, D. Keegan and B. Holmberg (Eds.), *Distance Education: International Perspectives*. London: Croom Helm.

Philips, P. (1991, March). Is industrial democracy feasible? Lessons from Mondragon. *Canadian Dimension*, 38–41.

Plowden Report (1967). *Children and their Primary Schools*. London: HMSO.

Quarter, J. (1995). *Crossing the Line: Unionized Employee Ownership and Investment Funds*. Toronto: Lorimer.

Razack, S. (1993). Teaching activists for social change: Coming to grips with questions of subjectivity and domination. *The Canadian Journal for the Study of Adult Education* 7(2) 43-56.

Richardson, M., Sherman, J. and Gismondi, M. (1993). *Winning Back the Words: Confronting Experts in an Environmental Public Hearing*. Toronto: Garamond Press.

Robertson, D., Rinehart, J. and Huxley, C. (1989). Team concept and Kaizen: Japanese production management in a unionised Canadian auto plant. *Studies in Political Economy* 39, 77–107.

Saul, N. (1994, January). *Organising the Organized*. Unpublished master's thesis, Warwick University, Coventry, England.

Sawchuk, P. (2003). On-line learning for union activists? Findings from a Canadian study. *Studies in Continuing Education 25* (1)

Schein, E. (1985). *Organizational Culture and Leadership*. San Francisco: Jossey-Bass.

Schultz, T.W. (1961). Investment in human capital. In M. Blaug, (Ed.) (1968). *Economics of Education*. London: Penguin.

Scott, S., Spencer, B. and Thomas, A. (1998). *Learning for Life: Canadian Readings in Adult Education*. Toronto: Thompson Educational.

Selman, G., Cooke, M., Selman, M. and Dampier, P. (1998). *The Foundations of Adult Education*. (2nd Ed.). Toronto: Thompson Educational.

Senge, P. (1990). The leader's new work: Building learning organizations. *Sloan Management Review*, Fall.

Sewart, D. (1983). Distance teaching: A contradiction in terms? In D. Sewart, D. Keegan and B. Holmberg (Eds.), *Distance Education: International Perspectives*. London: Croom Helm.

Shaffer, H.G. (1961). A critique of the concept of human capital. In M. Blaug, (Ed.) (1968), *Economics of Education,* London: Penguin, 45-57.

Sheehan, N. (1995). Sexism in education. In R. Ghosh and D. Ray (Eds.), *Social Change and Eduction in Canada*, (3rd Ed.). Toronto: Harcourt Brace, 323–341.

Shields, J. (1996). Flexible work, labour market polarization, and the politics of skills training and enhancement. In Dunk, T., McBride, S., and Nelsen, R. *The Training Trap: Ideology, Training and the Labour Market.* Halifax, NS: SSS/Fernwood Publishing.

Shrecker, T. (1993). *Sustainable Development: Getting There from Here.* Ottawa: CLC National Round Table on the Environment and the Economy.

Shrecker, T. (1994). Environmentalism and the politics of invisibility. *Alternatives* 20(2) 8–15.

Simon, B. (Ed.), (1990). *The Search for Enlightenment: The Working Class and Adult Education in the Twentieth Century.* London: Lawrence and Wishart.

Smith, D. (1975). An analysis of ideological structures and how women are excluded: Considerations for academic women. In J. Gaskel and A. McLaren (Eds.) (1988), *Women and Education: A Canadian Perspective.* Calgary: Detselig, 237–249.

Smith, D. (1987). *The Everyday World as Problematic: A Feminist Sociology.* Toronto: University of Toronto Press.

Spencer, B. (Ed.) (1986). *Adult Education with the Unemployed.* Leeds: University of Leeds.

Spencer, B. (1992). Labour education in the UK and Canada. *Canadian and International Education* 21(2) 55–68.

Spencer, B. (Ed.) (2002). *Unions and Learning in a Global Economy: International and Comparative Perspectives.* Toronto: Thompson Educational Publishing.

Spencer, B. (2002a). Research and the pedagogics of work and learning in *Journal of Workplace Learning 14,* (7). 298 – 305.

Spencer, B. (2004). Flexible learning. In G. Foley (ed.), *Dimensions of Adult Learning: Adult Education and Training in a Global Era.* Sydney: Allen and Unwin.

Spencer, B. and McIlroy, J. (1991). British university adult education in context. *Canadian Journal of University Continuing Education* (17)2.

Spencer, B., Briton, D., and Gereluk, W., (1999). From learning to credential: PLAR. *CASAE Conference,* University of Montreal, 190-195.

Spender, D. (1980). Learning to create our own knowledge. *Convergence* 13(1–2).

Spronk, B. (1994). Distance learning for participatory development: A case study. *Canadian Journal of University Continuing Education* 20(2) 9–22.

Storey, J. (2001). *Human Resource Management: A Critical Text (Second Edition).* London: Thomson Learning.

Swerdlow, M. (1990). *Brother Max: Labour Organizer and Educator.* St. John's: CCLH.

Swift, J. (1995). *Wheel of Fortune: Work and Life in the Age of Falling Expectations.* Toronto: Between the Lines.

Taylor, J. (1994). *Fashioning Farmers: Ideology, Agricultural Knowledge and the Manitoba Farm Movement, 1890–1925.* Regina: Canadian Plains Research Centre.

Taylor, J. (1996). The continental classroom: Teaching labour studies on-line. *Labor Studies Journal* 21(1) 19–38.

Taylor, J. (2001). *Union Learning: Canadian Labour Education in the Twentieth Century.* Toronto: Thompson Educational Publishing.

Taylor, M. (Ed.) (1997). *Workplace Education: The Changing Landscape.* Toronto: Culture Concepts.

Taylor, R. (1993). Continuing education and the accessible university. *University of Leeds Review* 36, 313–330.

Taylor, R. and Ward, K. (1986). *Adult Education and the Working Class: Education for the Missing Millions*. London: Croom Helm.

Taylor, R., Rockhill, K. and Fieldhouse, R. (1985). *University Adult Education in England and the USA*. London: Croom Helm.

Thomas, A. (1993). The new world of continuing education. In T. Barer-Stein and J. Draper, (Eds.), *The Craft of Teaching Adults*. Toronto: Culture Concepts, 21–38.

Thomas, A.M. (1991). *Beyond Education*. San Francisco: Jossey-Bass.

Thompson E.P. (1963). *The Making of the English Working Class*. London: Penguin.

Thompson, J. (1983). *Learning Liberation*. London: Croom Helm.

Thompson, J. (Ed.) (1980). *Adult Education for a Change*. London: Hutchinson.

University of Alberta (1992). *University of Alberta Senate Report*. Edmonton: Author.

Vector Public Education Inc. (1990, November). *Evaluation of Schools and Programs*. Ottawa: Author/ CLC Educational Services.

Vernon, F. (1960). *The Development of Adult Education in Ontario, 1790–1900*. Unpublished Ph.D. dissertation, University of Toronto.

Wallace, R. and Wolf, A. (1991). *Contemporary Sociological Theory: Continuing the Classical Tradition* (3rd Ed.). Englewood Cliffs, New Jersey: Prentice Hall.

Waters, M. (1994). *Modern Sociological Theory*. London: Sage.

Wellins, R. (1991). *Empowered Teams: Creating Self-directed Work Groups that Improve Quality, Productivity and Participation*. San Francisco: Jossey-Bass.

Welton, M. (1991). *Toward Development Work: The Workplace as a Learning Environment*. Geelong: Deakin University Press.

Welton, M. (1993). Social revolutionary learning: The new social movements as learning sites. *Adult Education Quarterly* 43(3) 152–165.

Welton, M. (1995). *In Defense of the Lifeworld: Critical Perspectives on Adult Learning*. New York: SUNY.

Welton, M. (2005). *Designing the Just Learning Society: A Critical Inquiry*. Leicester: NIACE.

Welton, M.R. (Ed.) (1987). *Knowledge for the People*. Toronto: OISE.

Whyte, W.F. and Whyte, K.K. (1988). *Making Mondragon*. Ithaca: IRL.

Wilkins, H. (1991). Computer talk: Long-distance conversations by computer. *Written Communication*, 8, 56-78.

Wiltshire. H. (1980). *The 1919 Report*. Nottingham: The Department of Adult Education University of Nottingham.

Wootherspoon, T. (2004). *The sociology of Education: Critical Perspectives*. Toronto: OUP.

Youngman, F. (1986). *Adult Education and Socialist Pedagogy*. London: Croom Helm.

Zachariah, M. (1986). *Revolution through Reform*. New York: Praeger.

Zukas, M. and Pillinger, J. (1990). Women, technology and adult education. *Industrial Tutor* 5(2) 28–42.

Index